Reservation in India

Recent Perspectives in Higher Education

Reservation in India

Recent Perspectives in Higher Education

Dr. Harpreet Kaur

Dr. R.K. Suri

PENTAGON PRESS

Reservation in India: Recent Perspectives in Higher Education /
Dr. R.K. Suri and Dr. Harpreet Kaur
Includes preface and index

ISBN 978-81-8274-403-5

First Published in 2009

Published by
PENTAGON PRESS
206, Peacock Lane, Shahpur Jat,
New Delhi-110049
Phones: 011-64706243, 26491568
Telefax: 011-26490600
email: rajan@pentagon-press.com
website: www.pentagon-press.com

Printed at
Syndicate Binders
A-20, Hosiery Complex, Noida Phase-II Extn., Noida-201305, U.P.

Preface

The minority groups in India have a long history of deprivation and disadvantage and its members being disproportionately under-represented amongst the upper socio-economic station is creating a new form of disparity and sowing the seeds of distrust and animosity between various communities. Discrimination proves dangerous for it retards expected progress of the society and it also deviates us from the path of development and planning.

A potent instrument used to bring out equality is granting socio-economic, religious and political concessions to the economically weaker sections. Such caste based reservations emphasize the fact that one has to mobilize on one's community identity if one wants to be heard, undermining one's capability to face competition on an individual basis. Eventually, we should do away with 'caste-based reservations' which not only spreads ill-will amongst the people but also promotes unhealthy competition.

A major debate is ongoing between the individual right to equal treatment and the societal goal of overcoming profound inequalities of opportunities. Backwardness is based more on individual characteristics and when based on caste, it tends to reward the wrong set of individuals. At this juncture, it is necessary to identify the set of people who need reservation not on the basis of group, but on individual basis.

Excellence and equity are twin objectives which we should aim at. But a major question remains that can equity really be achieved through reservations.

Social harmony can be established in the society if various marginalized groups are assimilated into the mainstream of the society and disparities can be removed by providing level playing field to the disadvantaged sections of the society. One of the major pre-requisites of good governance is minimization of disparity, elimination of discrimination and adequate representation to all segments of people from all walks of life.

Our family members have always been understanding and supportive and their constant encouragement has been a major factor which motivated us to pursue this work. We are extremely indebted to Dr. Jaspal Singh, Vice-Chancellor, Punjabi University, Patiala for his impetus providing inspiration. We are also thankful to Dr. J.B. Singh, Principal, Sri Guru Gobind Singh College of Commerce, University of Delhi, and colleagues.

Comments and suggestions are highly appreciated.

Dr. Harpreet Kaur

Dr. R.K. Suri

Contents

CHAPTER 1

Caste, Class and Discrimination

Social inequality in many other nations across the globe are predominantly noticed, but nowhere else in the world has social inequality been so elaborately constructed in the social fabric as in the Indian institution of caste. Caste has long existed in India, however, in the modern period it has been severely criticized by both Indian and foreign observers from time to time in their writings. Although some educated Indians tell non-Indians that caste has been abolished or that *"no one pays attention to caste anymore,"* such statements often do not reflect true reality.

The term caste has been derived from the Portuguese term 'caste' which means race, breed or kind. M.N. Srinivas says, "A sociologist would define caste as a hereditary endogamous, usually localized group, having a traditional association with an occupation and a particular positions in the local hierarchy of castes. Relations between castes are governed, among other things by the concepts of pollution and generally commonality occurs within the caste."

Caste and Varna system has undergone significant changes ever since introduction of English as a medium of instruction and more so after independence, however it still affects the lives of hundreds of millions of people. In its Preamble, Indian Constitution forbids negative public discrimination on the basis of caste. However, caste ranking and caste based interaction have 'occurred for centuries and will continue to do so well into the foreseeable future, more in the countryside than in urban settings and more in the realms of kinship and closed community marriage than in less personal interactions. Caste and Varna is still a form of stratification of class in the society.

The castes are named as endogamous (in-marrying) groups, membership in which is achieved by birth. There are thousands of castes and sub-castes in India, and these large 'kinship-based' groups are fundamental to South Asian social structure. Each caste is part of a locally based system of interdependence with other groups, involving occupational specialization, and is linked in complex ways with networks that stretch across regions and throughout the nation. However, the traditional castes based on occupational specialization is disappearing fast due to rapid urbanization, industrialization and globalisation.

The word *caste* is derived from the Portuguese word *casta*, meaning breed, race, or kind. Among the Indian terms that are sometimes translated as caste are *varna, jati, jat, biradri,* and *sarna.* All of these terms refer to ranked groups of various sizes and breadth. *Varna,* or color, actually refers to large divisions that include various castes; the other terms include castes and sub-divisions of castes sometimes called sub-castes.

Many castes are traditionally associated with an occupation, such as high-ranking Brahmans warrior community as Kshatryias, middle-ranking farmers and trading community labelled as Vaishayas and artisan groups, such as potters, barbars, and carpenters and very low-ranking "Untouchable" or Shudras such as leatherworkers, butchers, launderers, and latrine cleaners and some castes are backward in terms of social and economic criteria. There is some correlation between ritual rank on the caste hierarchy and economic prosperity. Members of higher-ranking castes tend, on the whole, to be more prosperous than members of lower-ranking castes. Many lower-caste people live in conditions of abject poverty and social disadvantage.

According to Indian Holy Scriptures, the Rig Veda and the sacred texts that date back to old traditions of more than 3,000 years ago, progenitors of the four ranked varna groups sprang from various parts of the body of the primordial man, which Brahma created from clay. Each group had a function in sustaining the life of society—the social body. Brahmans, or priests, were created from the mouth. They were to provide for the intellectual and spiritual needs of the community. Kshatriyas, warriors and rulers, were derived from the arms. Their role was to rule and to protect others. Vaishyas—landowners and merchants—sprang from the thighs, and were entrusted with the care of commerce and agriculture. Shudras—artisans and servants—came from the feet. Their task was to perform all manual labour.

Later was a fifth category conceptualized "Untouchable" menials, relegated to carrying out very menial and polluting work related to bodily decay and dirt. Since 1935 "Untouchables" have been known as Scheduled Castes, referring to their listing on government rosters, or schedules. They were often called by Mohandas Karamchand (Mahatma) Gandhi as Harijans, or "Children of God." Although the term *Untouchable* appears in literature produced by these low-ranking castes, in the 1990s, many politically conscious members of these groups prefer to refer to themselves as Dalit, a Hindi word meaning oppressed or downtrodden. According to the 1991 census, there were 138,223,277 Scheduled Caste members in India, approximately 16.48 per cent of the total population; there were 67,758,380 Scheduled Tribes which constitute 8.08 per cent of total population. The State with highest proportion of Scheduled Castes is Punjab (28.3 per cent) and the State with lowest proportion of Scheduled Castes is Mizoram (0.1 per cent). The State with highest proportion of Scheduled Tribes is Mizoram (94.8 per cent) and the State with lowest proportion of Scheduled Tribes is Uttar Pradesh (0.2 per cent).

As per the historical records the first four *varnas* apparently existed in the ancient Aryan society of northern India. However, some historians say that these categories were originally somewhat fluid functional groups, and not castes. A greater degree of fixity gradually developed, resulting in the complex ranking systems of medieval India that essentially continued in the late twentieth century.

Although a *varna* is not a caste, when directly asked for their caste affiliation, particularly when the questioner is a Westerner, many Indians will reply with a *varna* name. Pressed further, they may respond with a much more specific name of a caste, or *jati*, which falls within that *varna*. For example, a Brahman may specify that he is a member of a named caste group, such as a Jijotiya Brahman, or a Smartha Brahman, and so on. Within such castes, people may further belong to smaller subcaste categories and to specific clans and lineages. These finer designations are particularly relevant when marriages are being arranged and often appear in newspaper matrimonial advertisements.

Members of a caste are typically spread out over a region, with representatives living in hundreds of settlements. In any small village, there may be representatives of a few or even a score or more castes.

Numerous groups usually called as tribes (often referred to as Scheduled Tribes) are also integrated into the caste system to varying degrees. Some tribes live separately from others—particularly in the far northeast and in the forested centre of the country, where tribes are more like ethnic groups than castes. Some tribes are themselves divided into groups similar to subcastes. In regions where members of tribes live in peasant villages with non-tribal peoples, they are usually considered members of separate castes ranking low on the hierarchical scale.

The inequalities among castes are considered by the Hindu faith to be part of the divinely ordained natural order and are expressed in terms of purity and pollution. Within a village, relative rank is most graphically expressed at a wedding or death feast, when all residents of the village are invited and also in terms of access to education system. At the home of a high-ranking caste member, food is prepared by a member of a caste from whom all can accept cooked food (usually by a Brahman). Diners are seated in lines; members of a single caste sit next to each other in a row, and members of other castes sit in perpendicular or parallel rows at some distance. Members of Dalit castes, such as Leatherworkers and Sweepers, may be seated far from the other diners—even out in an alley. Farther away, at the edge of the feeding area, a Sweeper may wait with a large basket to receive discarded leavings tossed in by other diners. Eating food contaminated by contact with the saliva of others not of the same family is considered far too polluting to be practiced by members of any other castes. Generally, feasts and ceremonies given by Dalits are not attended by higher-ranking castes.

Among the Muslims, although status differences prevail, brotherhood may be greatly stressed as per the religious prescriptions. A Muslim feast usually includes a cloth laid either of clean ground or on a table, with all Muslims, rich and poor, dining from plates placed on the same cloth. Muslims who wish to provide hospitality to observant Hindus, however, must make separate arrangements for a high-caste Hindu cook and ritually pure foods and dining area.

Castes that fall within the top four ranked *varnas* are sometimes referred to as the "clean castes," with Dalits considered "unclean." Castes of the top three ranked *varnas* are often designated "twice-born," in reference to the ritual initiation undergone by male members, in which investiture with the Hindu sacred thread constitutes a kind of ritual rebirth. Non-Hindu caste like groups generally fall outside these designations.

Each caste is believed by devout Hindus to have its own dharma, or divinely ordained code of proper conduct. Accordingly, there is often a high degree of tolerance for divergent lifestyles among different castes. Brahmans are usually expected to be nonviolent and spiritual, according to their traditional roles as vegetarian teetotaller priests. Kshatriyas are supposed to be strong, as fighters and rulers should be, with a taste for aggression, eating meat, and drinking alcohol. Vaishyas are stereotyped as adept businessmen, in accord with their traditional activities in commerce. Shudras are often described by others as tolerably pleasant but expectably somewhat base in behaviour, whereas Dalits—especially Sweepers—are often regarded by others as followers of vulgar life-styles. Conversely, lower-caste people often view people of high rank as haughty and unfeeling.

The chastity of women is strongly related to caste status. Generally, the higher ranking the caste, the more sexual control its women are expected to exhibit. Brahman brides should be virginal, faithful to one husband and celibate in widowhood. On the contrast, a Sweeper bride may or may not be virgin, extramarital affairs may be tolerated, and, if widowed or divorced, the woman is encouraged to remarry. For the higher castes, such control of female sexuality helps ensure purity of lineage—of crucial importance to maintenance of high status. Among Muslims, too, high status is strongly correlated with female chastity.

Within the castes explicit standards are invariably maintained. Transgressions may be dealt with by a caste council *(panchayat)*, meeting periodically to adjudicate issues relevant to the caste. Such councils are usually formed of groups of elders, almost always males. Punishments such as fines and out casting, either temporary or permanent, can be enforced. In rare cases, a person is excommunicated from the caste for gross infractions of caste rules. An example of such an infraction might be marrying or openly cohabiting with a mate of a caste lower than one's own; such behaviour would usually result in the higher-caste person dropping to the status of the lower-caste person.

The activities such as farming or trading can be carried out by anyone, but usually only members of the appropriate castes act as priests, barbars, potters, weavers, and other skilled artisans, whose occupational skills are handed down in families from one generation to another. As with other key features of Indian social structure, occupational specialization is believed to be in accord with the divinely ordained order of the universe.

The existence of rigid ranking is supernaturally validated through the idea of rebirth according to a person's karma, the sum of an individual's deeds in this life and in past lives. After death, a person's life is judged by divine forces, and rebirth is assigned in a high or a low place, depending upon what is deserved. This supernatural sanction can never be neglected, because it brings a person to his or her position in the caste hierarchy, relevant to every transaction involving food or drink, speaking, or touching.

In past decades, Dalits in certain areas (especially in parts of the south) had to display extreme deference to high-status people, physically keeping their distance—best their touch or even their shadow pollute others—wearing neither shoes nor any upper body covering (even for women) in the presence of the upper castes. The lowest-ranking had to jingle a little bell in warning of their polluting approach. In large part of India, Dalits were prohibited from entering temples, or using wells from which the "clean" castes drew their water, or even attending schools. In past centuries, dire punishments were prescribed for Dalits who read or even heard sacred texts. However, such degrading discrimination was made illegal under legislation passed during British rule and was protested against by pre-independence reform movements led by Mahatma Gandhi, Sir Phule and Bhimrao Ramji (B.R.) Ambedkar, a Dalit leader. Dalits agitated for the right to enter Hindu temples and to use village wells and effectively pressed for the enactment of stronger laws opposing disabilities imposed on them. After independence, Ambedkar almost single-handedly wrote India's Constitution, including key provisions barring caste-based discrimination. Nonetheless, discriminatory treatment of Dalits remains a factor in daily life, especially in villages, even in the twenty first century.

In modern times, as it is virtually impossible for an individual to raise his own status by falsely claiming to be a member of a higher-ranked caste. Such a ruse might work for a time in a place where the person is unknown, but no one would dine with or intermarry with such a person or his offspring until the claim was validated through kinship networks. Rising on the ritual hierarchy can only be achieved by a caste as a group, over a long period of time, principally by adopting behaviour patterns of higher ranked groups. This process, known as Sanskritization, has been described by M.N. Srinivas and others. An example of such behaviour is that of some Leatherworker castes adopting a policy of not eating beef, in the hope that abstaining from the defiling practice of consuming the flesh of sacred bovines would enhance their castes' status. Increased economic prosperity for much of a caste greatly aids in the process of improving rank.

INTERCASTE RELATIONS AND JAJMANI SYSTEM

In a village, members of different castes are often linked in what has been referred as the *jajmani* system, after the word *jajman*, which in some regions means patron. Members of various service castes perform tasks for their patrons, usually members of the dominant, that is, most powerful landowning caste of the village (commonly castes of the Kshatriya *varna*). Households of service castes are linked through hereditary bonds to a household of patrons, with the lower-caste members providing services according to traditional occupational specializations. Thus, client families of launderers, barbars, shoemakers, carpenters, potters, tailors, and priests provide customary services to their patrons, in return for which they receive customary seasonal payments of grain, clothing, and money. Ideally, from generation to generation, clients owe their patrons political allegiance in addition to their labours, while patrons owe their clients protection and social security.

The harmonious qualities of the *jajmani* system have been over idealized and variations of the system overlooked by many observers. Further, the economic interdependence of the system has weakened since the 1960s. Nevertheless, it is clear that members of different castes customarily perform a number of functions for one another in rural India that emphasizes cooperation rather than competition. This cooperation is revealed in economic arrangements, in visits to farmers' threshing floors by service caste members to claim traditional payments, and in rituals emphasizing interdependence at life crisis and calendrical festivals all-over South Asia. For example, in rural Karnataka, in an event described by anthropologist Suzanne Hanchett, the annual procession of the village temple cart bearing images of the deities responsible for the welfare of the village cannot go forward without the combined efforts of representatives of all castes. It is believed that the sacred cart will literally not move unless all work together to move it, some pushing and some pulling.

However, some observers feel that the caste system must be viewed as a system of exploitation of poor low-ranking groups by more prosperous high-ranking groups. In many parts of India, land is largely held by dominant castes—high-ranking owners of property—that economically exploit low-ranking landless labourers and poor artisans, all the while degrading them with ritual emphasis on their so-called god-given inferior status. In the early 1990s, blatant subjugation of low-caste labourers in the northern state of Bihar and in eastern Uttar Pradesh was the subject of many news reports. In this region, scores of Dalits who have attempted to unite in the form of Ranveer Sena or other such groups, to protest low wages have been the victims of lynching and mass killings by high-caste landowners and their hired assassins.

In 1991 the news magazine *India Today* reported that in an ostensibly prosperous village about 160 kilometres southeast of Delhi, when it became known that a rural Dalit labourer dared to have a love affair with the daughter of a high-caste landlord, the lovers and their Dalit go-between were tortured, publicly hanged, and burnt by agents of the girl's family in the presence of some 500 villagers. A similar incident occurred in 1994, when a Dalit musician who had secretly married a woman of the Kurmi cultivating caste was beaten to death by outraged Kurmis, possibly instigated by the young woman's family. The terrified bride was stripped and branded, as a punishment for her transgression. Dalit women also have been the victims of gang rapes by the police or armed forces. Many other atrocities, as well as urban riots resulting in the deaths of Dalits, have occurred in recent years. Such extreme injustices are infrequent enough to be reported in outraged articles in the Indian press, while much more common daily discrimination and exploitation are considered virtually routine.

SIGNIFICANT CHANGES IN THE CASTE SYSTEM

Inspite of various problems, the caste system has operated quite successfully for centuries, providing goods and services to millions of Indian citizens. The system continues to operate, but changes are occurring. India's Constitution guarantees basic rights to all its citizens, including the right to equality and equal protection before the law. The practice of untouchability, as well as discrimination on the basis of caste, race, sex, or religion, has been legally abolished. All citizens have the right to vote, and political competition is lively. Voters from every stratum of society have formed interest groups, overlapping and crosscutting castes, creating and evolving new style of integrating Indian society.

Castes themselves, however, far from being abolished, have certain rights under Indian law. As described by anthropologist Owen M. Lynch and other scholars, in the expanding political arena caste groups are becoming more politicized and forced to compete with other interest groups for social and economic benefits. In the growing cities, traditional intercaste interdependencies are negligible.

Independent India has built on earlier British efforts to remedy problems suffered by Dalits by granting them some benefits of protective discrimination. Scheduled Castes are entitled to reserve electoral offices, reserved jobs in central and state governments, and special educational benefits. The Constitution mandates that one-seventh of state and national legislative seats should be reserved for members of Scheduled Castes in order to guarantee their voice in government. Reserving seats has proven useful because few, if any, Scheduled Caste candidates have ever been elected in non-reserved constituencies.

It is interesting to note that educationally, Dalit students have benefited from scholarships, and Scheduled Caste literacy increased (from 10.3 per cent in 1961 to 21.4 per cent in 1981, the last year for which such figures are available), although not as rapidly as among the general population as many dalits are still looking out for traditional vocational activities and the education has not provided them with better job prospects. Improved access to education has resulted in the emergence of a substantial group of educated Dalits who are able to take up white-collar occupations and fight for their rights. However, this is true only for selected few.

There has been tremendous resistance among non-Dalits to this protective discrimination for the Scheduled Castes, who constitute some 16 per cent of the total population. Also efforts have been made to provide similar advantages to the so-called Backward Classes who constitute an estimated 52 per cent of the population. In August 1990, Prime Minister Vishwanath Pratap (V.P.) Singh announced his intention to enforce the recommendations of the Backward Classes Commission (Mandal Commission), issued in December 1980 and largely ignored for a decade. The report, which urged special advantages for obtaining government jobs, civil service positions and admission to higher and technical education for the Backward Classes, resulted in riots and self-immolations (Rajeev Goswami Case) by the members of upper castes and contributed to the fall of the prime minister. The upper castes have been particularly adamant against these policies because unemployment is a major problem in India, and many feel that they are being unjustly excluded from posts for which they are better qualified than lower-caste applicants.

As an act of protest, many Dalits have rejected Hinduism with its rigid ranking system. Following the example of their revered leader, Dr. Ambedkar, who converted to Buddhism four years before his death in 1956, millions of Dalits have embraced the faith of the Buddha. Over the past few centuries, many Dalits have also converted to Christianity and have often by this means raised their socio-economic status. However, Christians of Dalit origin often suffer from discrimination by Christians—and others—of higher caste backgrounds.

Despite some improvements in some aspects of Dalit status, 90 per cent of them lived in rural areas in the mid-1990s, where an increasing proportion—more than 50 percent—worked as landless agricultural labourers. State and national governments have attempted to secure more just distribution of land by creating land ceilings and abolishing absentee landlordism, but evasive tactics by landowners have successfully prevented more than minimal redistribution of land to tenant farmers and labourers. In contemporary India, field hands face increased competition from tractors and harvesting machines. Similarly, artisans are being challenged by expanding commercial markets in mass-produced factory goods, undercutting traditional mutual obligations between patrons and clients. The spread of the Green Revolution has tended to increase the gap between the prosperous and the poor—most of whom are low-caste. The growth of urbanization (an estimated 26 per cent of the population now lives in cities and many of them in upcoming metropolitan cities) is having a far-reaching effect on caste practices, not only in cities but in villages. Among anonymous crowds in urban public spaces and on public transportation, caste affiliations are unknown, and observance of purity and pollution rules is considered to be negligible. Distinctive caste customs have all but vanished, and low-caste names have been modified, although castes remain endogamous, and access to employment often occurs through intracaste connections. Various restrictions on interactions with other castes are becoming more relaxed, and, at the same time, observance of other pollution rules is declining—especially those concerning birth, death, and menstruation on account of mobility. Several growing Hindu sects draw members from many castes and regions, and communication between cities and villages is expanding dramatically. Kin in town and country visit one another frequently, and television programs available to huge numbers of villagers vividly portray new lifestyles. Further, rapid infrastructure development in terms of Malls, Retails, Highways, Metros etc. have also has resulted in changes in activities, attitudes and life styles. As new occupations open up in urban areas, Predominantly call centres and IT enabled service, the correlation of caste with occupation is declining.

Caste associations have expanded their areas of concern beyond traditional elite emulation and local politics into the wider political arenas of state and national politics. Finding power in numbers within India's democratic system, caste groups are pulling together closely allied sub-castes in their quest for political influence. In efforts to solidify caste bonds, some caste associations have organized marriage fairs where families can make matches for their children. Traditional hierarchical concerns are being minimized in favour of strengthening horizontal unity. Thus, while pollution observances are declining, caste consciousness is not.

Education and election to political office have advanced the status of many Dalits, but the overall picture remains one of great inequity. In recent decades, Dalit anger has been expressed in writings, demonstrations, strikes, and the activities of such groups as the Dalit Panthers, a radical political party demanding revolutionary change. A wider Dalit movement, including political parties, educational activities, self-help centres, and labour organizations, has spread to many areas of the country. The growth and development of Bahujan Samaj Party, a party of Dalit has also helped in the emancipation of Dalits.

In a 1982 Dalit publication, Dilip Hiro wrote, "It is one of the great modern Indian tragedies and dangers that even well meaning Indians still find it so difficult to accept. Untouchable mobility as being legitimate in fact as well as in theory. . . ." Still, against all odds, a small intelligentsia has worked for many years towards the goal of freeing India of caste consciousness.

THE CLASSES IN INDIAN SOCIETY

In India's villages, where nearly 74 per cent of the population resides, caste and class affiliations overlap. According to anthropologist Miriam Sharma, "Large landholders who employ hired labour are overwhelmingly from the upper castes, while the agricultural workers themselves come from the ranks of the lowest—predominantly Untouchable—castes." She also points out that household-labour-using proprietors come from the ranks of the middle agricultural castes. Distribution of other resources and access to political control follow the same pattern of caste-cum-class distinctions. Although this congruence is strong, there is a tendency for class formation to occur despite the importance of caste, especially in the cities, but also in rural areas.

In an analysis of class formation in India, anthropologist Harold A. Gould states that a three level system of stratification is taking shape across rural India. He calls the three levels—Forward Classes (higher castes), Backward Classes (middle and lower castes), and Harijans (very low castes). Members of these groups share common concerns because they stand in approximately the same relationship to land and production—that is, they are large-scale farmers, small-scale farmers, and landless labourers. Some of these groups are drawing together within regions across caste lines in order to work for political power and access to desirable resources. For example, since the late 1960s, some of the middle ranking cultivating castes of northern India have increasingly cooperated in the political arena in order to advance their common agrarian and market-oriented interests. Their efforts have been spurred by competition with higher-caste landed elites.

On the other hand, cities other groups have vested interests which cut across the caste in boundaries, suggesting the possibility of forming classes in the future. These groups include prosperous industrialists and entrepreneurs, who have made successful efforts to push the central government towards a pro-business stance; bureaucrats, who depend upon higher education rather than land to preserve their positions as civil servants; political officeholders, who enjoy good salaries and perquisites of all kinds; and the military, who constitute one of the most powerful armed forces in the developing world. Economically far below such groups are members of the menial underclass, which is taking shape in both villages and urban areas. As the privileged elites move ahead, low-ranking menial workers remain economically insecure. Were they to join together to mobilize politically across lines of class and religion in recognition of their common interests, Gould observes, they might find power in their sheer numbers.

India's rapidly expanding and growing economy has provided the basis for a fundamental change—the emergence of what an eminent journalist Suman Dubey calls a *"new vanguard"* increasingly dictating India's new political and economic direction. This group is referred as India's new middle class—mobile, driven, consumer-oriented, and, to some extent, forward-looking and politically conscious of its rights. Hard to define precisely, it is not a single stratum of society, but straddles town and countryside, making its voice heard everywhere. It encompasses prosperous farmers, white-collar workers business people, military personnel, and myriad others, all actively working towards a prosperous life. Ownership of cars, televisions, computers and other consumer goods, reasonable earnings, substantial savings, and educated children (often fluent in English) typify this diverse group. Many have ties to kinsmen, who are living abroad and who have done very well in Middle East or North America.

The new middle class is booming, at least partially in response to perequisites doubling of the salaries of some 4 million central government employees in 1986, followed by similar increases for state and district officers. Unprecedented liberalization and opening up of the economy in the 1980s and 1990s have been part of the picture. There is no single set of criteria defining the middle class, and estimates of its numbers vary widely. The midrange of figures presented in a 1992 survey article by analyst Suman Dubey is approximately 150 to 175 million—some 20 per cent of the population—although other observers suggest alternative figures. The middle class appears to be increasing rapidly. Once primarily urban and largely Hindu, the phenomenon of the consuming middle class is burgeoning among Muslims and prosperous villagers as well. According to V.A. Pai Panandikar, former director of the Centre for Policy Research, New Delhi, cited by Dubey, by the end of the twentieth century 30 per cent—some 300 million—of India's population will be middle class. The middle class is also travelling widely abroad and in India.

The middle class is bracketed on either side by the upper and lower echelons. Members of the upper class—around 1 per cent of the population—are owners of large properties, members of exclusive clubs, and vacationers in foreign lands, and include industrialists, former maharajas, and top executives. Below the middle class is perhaps a third of the population—ordinary farmers, traders, artisans, and workers. At the bottom of the economic scale are the poor—estimate at 320 million, some 45 per cent of the population in 1988—who live in inadequate homes without adequate food, work for pittances, have undereducated and often have malnourished children, and are victims of numerous social inequities.

THE SIGNIFICANT OTHERS (FRINGES) OF SOCIETY

India's complex society comprises some unique members—sadhus (holy men) and *hijras* (transvestite-eunuchs) etc. Such people have voluntarily stepped outside the usual bonds of kinship and caste to join with others in caste like groups based upon personal—yet culturally shaped—inclinations. In India of the 1990s, several hundred thousand Hindu and Jain sadhus and a few thousand holy women (*sadhvis*) lived, an ascetic life. They have chose to wear ochre robes, or perhaps no clothing at all, to daub their skin with holy ash, to pray and meditate, and to wander from place to place, depending on the charity of others. Most have given up affiliation with their caste and kin and have undergone a funeral ceremony for themselves, followed by a ritual rebirth into their new ascetic life. They come from all walks of life, and range from illiterate villagers to well-educated professionals. In their new lives as renunciants, they are devoted to spiritual concerns, yet each is affiliated with an ascetic order or sub sect demanding strict adherence to rules of dress, itinerancy, diet, worship, and ritual pollution. Within each order, hierarchical concerns are exhibited in the subservience novitiates display to revered gurus. Further, at pilgrimage sites, different orders take precedence in accordance with an accepted hierarchy. Thus, although sadhus have foresworn many of the trappings of ordinary life, they have not given up the hierarchy and interdependence so pervasive in Indian society.

The most extreme sadhus, the *aghoris,* turn normal rules of conduct completely upside down. Rajesh and Ramesh Bedi, who have studied sadhus for decades, estimate that there may be fewer than fifteen *aghoris* in contemporary India. In the quest for great spiritual attainment, the *aghori* lives alone, like Lord Shiva, at cremation grounds, supping from a human skull bowl. He eats food provided only by low-ranking Sweepers and prostitutes, and in moments of religious fervour devours his own bodily wastes and pieces of human flesh torn from burning corpses. In violating the most basic taboos of the ordinary Hindu householder, the *aghori sadhu* graphically reminds himself and others of the correct rules of social behaviour.

Hijras are males who have become "neither man nor woman," transsexual transvestites who are usually castrated and are attributed with certain ritual powers of blessing. As described by anthropologist Serena Nanda, they are distinct from ordinary male homosexuals (known as *zenana,* woman, or *anmarad,* un-man), who retain their identity as males and continue to live in ordinary society. Most *hijras* derive from a middle- or lower-status Hindu or Muslim background and have experienced male impotency or effeminacy. A few originally had ambiguous or hermaphroditic sexual organs. An estimated 50,000 *hijras* live throughout India, predominantly in cities of the north. They are united in the worship of the Hindu goddess Bahuchara Mata.

Hijras voluntarily leave their families of birth, renounce male sexuality, and assume a female identity, name, and dress. A *hijra* undergoes a surgical emasculation in which he is transformed from an impotent male into a potentially powerful new person. Like Shiva—attributed with breaking off his phallus and throwing it to earth, thereby extending his sexual power to the universe (recognized in Hindu worship of the lingam)—the emasculated *hijra* has the power to bless others with fertility. Groups of *hijras* go about together, dancing and singing at the homes of new baby boys, blessing them with virility and the ability to continue the family line. *Hijras* are also attributed with the power to bring rain in times of drought. *Hijras* receive alms and respect for their powers, yet they are also ridiculed and abused because of their unusual sexual condition and because some act as male prostitutes.

The *hijra* community functions much like a caste. They have communal households; newly formed fictive kinship bonds, marriage-like arrangements; and seven nationwide "houses," or symbolic descent groups, with regional and national leaders, and a council. There is a hierarchy of gurus and disciples, with expulsion from the community a possible punishment for failure to obey group rules. Thus, although living on the margins of society, *hijras* are empowered by their special relationship with their goddess and each other and occupy an accepted and meaningful place in India's social world.

CASTE-BASED PARTIES

One irony of Indian politics is that its modern secular democracy has enhanced rather than reduced the political salience of traditional forms of social identity such as caste. Part of the explanation for this development is that India's political parties have found the caste-based selection of candidates and appeals to the caste-based interests of the Indian electorate to be an effective way to win popular support. More fundamental has been the economic development and social mobility of those groups officially designated as Backward Classes and Scheduled Castes. Accounting for 52 and 15 per cent of the population, respectively, the Backward Classes and Scheduled Castes, or Dalits as they prefer to be called, constitute a diverse range of middle, lower, and outcaste groups who have come to wield substantial power in most states. Indeed, one of the highlights of modern Indian politics has been the Backward Classes and Dalits' jettisoning of their political subordination to upper castes and their assertion of their own interests.

The Backward Classes are such a substantial constituency that almost all parties vie for their support. For instance, the Congress (I) in Maharashtra has long relied on Backward Classes' backing for its political success. The 1990s have seen a growing number of cases where parties, relying primarily on Backward Classes' support, often in alliance with Dalits and Muslims, catapult to power in India's states. Janata Dal governments in Bihar and Karnataka are excellent examples of this strategy. An especially important development is the success of the Samaj wadi Party, which under the leadership of Mulayam Singh Yadav won the 1993 assembly elections in India's most populous state, Uttar Pradesh, relying almost exclusively on Backward Classes and Muslim support in a coalition with the Dalit-supported BSP.

The growing support of the BSP also reflects the importance of caste-based politics and the assertiveness of the Dalits in particular. The BSP was founded by Kanshi Ram on April 14, 1984, the birthday of B.R. Ambedkar and draws inspiration from the teachings of Dr. Ambedkar. They also criticise Manu samiti which is the basis of hierarchical social order. Born as a Dalit in Punjab, Kanshi Ram resigned from his position as a government employee in 1964 and, after working in various political positions, founded the All-India Backward, Scheduled Caste, Scheduled Tribe, Other Backward Classes, and Minority Communities Employees Federation (BAMCEF) in 1978 whose main task was protection against caste discrimination. Kanshi Ram's assumption was that the sections responsible for oppression of dalits were in a minority and the Scheduled Castes, Scheduled Tribes, the backward castes and minorities and who have been oppressed constitute 85 per cent of the population constitute the 'Bahujan'. BSP leadership has mobilized the Scheduled Castes, the Scheduled Tribes, the other backward castes and other religious minorities on a common platform of 'Bahujan' and it is their ideological cum-electoral strategy.

Although both the BAMCEF and BSP pursue strategies of building support among Backward Classes, Scheduled Tribes, and Muslims as well as Dalits, Kanshi Ram has been most successful in building support among the Dalit Chamar (Leather worker) caste in North India. In the November 1993, Uttar Pradesh state elections, Ram's BSP achieved the best showing of any Dalit-based party by winning sixty-seven seats. At the same time, the BSP increased its representation in the Madhya Pradesh state legislature from two to twelve seats. On June 1, 1995, the BSP withdrew from the state government of Uttar Pradesh and, with the support of the BJP, formed a new government, making its leader, Mayawati, the first Dalit women ever to become a chief minister of Uttar Pradesh. The alliance, however, was seen by observers as doomed because of political differences. And the party has to a large extent failed to achieve its ambitions because of the internal problems and controversies, mainly the feudal and undemocratic behaviour of Kanshi Ram and Mayawati and use of arrogant and abusive language against the upper caste, etc.

THEMES IN INDIAN SOCIETY

India is a hierarchical society. Within Indian culture, whether in the north or the south, Hindu or Muslim, urban or rural areas, virtually all things, people, and groups of people are ranked according to various essential qualities. If one is attuned to the theme of hierarchy in India, one can discern it everywhere. Although India is a political democracy, in daily life there is little advocacy of or adherence to notions of equality.

Castes and caste like groups—those quintessential groups with which almost all Indians are associated—are ranked. Within most villages or towns, everyone knows the relative rankings of each locally represented caste, and people's behaviour towards one another is constantly shaped by this knowledge. Between the extremes of the very high and very low castes, however, there is sometimes disagreement on the exact relative ranking of castes clustered in the middle.

Castes are primarily associated with Hinduism but also exist among other Indian religious groups. Muslims sometimes expressly deny that they have castes—they state that all Muslims are brothers under God—but observation of Muslim life in various parts of India reveals the existence of caste like groups and clear concern with social hierarchy. Among Indian Christians, too, differences in caste are acknowledged and maintained.

Throughout India, individuals are also ranked according to their wealth and power. For example, there are "big men" *(bare admi,* in Hindi) and "little men" *(chhote admi*) everywhere. "Big men" sit confidently on chairs, while "little men" come before them to make requests, either standing or crouching down on their haunches, certainly not presuming to sit beside a man of high status as an equal. Even men of nearly equal status who might share a string cot to sit on take their places carefully—the higher-ranking man at the head of the cot, the lower-ranking man at the foot.

Within families and kinship groupings, there are many distinctions of hierarchy. Men outrank women of the same or similar age, and senior relatives outrank junior relatives. Several other kinship relations involve formal respect. For example, in northern India, a daughter-in-law of a household shows deference to a daughter of a household. Even among young siblings in a household, there is constant acknowledgment of age differences, younger siblings never address an older sibling by name, but rather by respectful terms for elder brother or elder sister. However, an older sibling may address the younger by name.

Even in a business or academic setting, where colleagues may not openly espouse traditional observance of caste or class ranking behaviour, they may set up fictive kinship relations, addressing one another by kinship terms reflecting family or village-style hierarchy. For example, a younger colleague might respectfully address an older colleague as *chachaji* (respected father's younger brother), gracefully acknowledging the superior position of the older colleague.

PURITY AND POLLUTION

Many status differences in Indian society are expressed in terms of ritual purity and pollution. Notions of purity and pollution are extremely complex and vary greatly among different castes, religious groups, and regions. However, broadly speaking, high status is associated with purity and low status with pollution. Some kinds of purity are inherent, or inborn; for example, gold is purer than copper by its very nature and, similarly, a member of a high-ranking Brahman or priest, caste is born with more inherent purity than a member of a low-ranking Sweeper (Mehtar, in Hindi) caste. Unless the Brahman defiles himself in some extraordinary way, throughout his life he will always be purer than a Sweeper. Other kinds of purity are more transitory—a Brahman who has just taken a bath is more ritually pure than a Brahman who has not bathed for a day. This situation could easily reverse itself temporarily, depending on bath schedules, participation in polluting activities, or contact with temporarily polluting substances.

Purity is associated with ritual cleanliness—daily bathing in flowing water, dressing in properly laundered clothes of approved materials, eating only the foods appropriate for one's caste, refraining from physical contact with people of lower rank, and avoiding involvement with ritually impure substances. The latter include body wastes and excretions, most especially those of another adult person. Contact with the products of death or violence are typically polluting and threatening to ritual purity.

During her menstrual period, a woman is considered polluted and refrains from cooking, worshipping, or touching anyone older than an infant. In much of the south, a woman spends this time "sitting outside," resting in an isolated room or shed. During her period, a Muslim woman does not touch the Quran. At the end of the period, purity is restored with a complete bath. Pollution also attaches to birth, both for the mother and the infant's close kin, and to death, for close relatives of the deceased. Members of the highest priestly castes, the Brahmans, are generally vegetarians (although some Bengali and Maharashtrian Brahmans eat fish) and avoid eating meat, the product of violence and death. High-ranking Warrior castes (Kshatriyas), however, typically consume non-vegetarian diets, considered appropriate for their traditions of valor and physical strength.

A Brahman born of proper Brahman parents retains his inherent purity if he bathes and dresses himself properly, adheres to a vegetarian diet, eats meals prepared only by persons of appropriate rank, and keeps his person away from the bodily exuviae of others (except for necessary contact with the secretions of family infants and small children).

If a Brahman happens to come into bodily contact with a polluting substance, he can remove this pollution by bathing and changing his clothing. However, if he were to eat meat or commit other transgressions of the rigid dietary codes of his particular caste, he would be considered more deeply polluted and would have to undergo various purifying rites and payment of fines imposed by his caste council in order to restore his inherent purity.

In sharp contrast to the purity of a Brahman, a Sweeper born of Sweeper parents is considered to be born inherently polluted. The touch of his body is polluting to those higher on the caste hierarchy than he, and they will shrink from his touch, whether or not he has bathed recently. Sweepers are associated with the traditional occupation of cleaning human faeces from latrines and sweeping public lanes of all kinds of dirt. Traditionally, Sweepers remove these polluting materials in baskets carried atop the head and dumped out in a garbage pile at the edge of the village or neighbourhood. The involvement of Sweepers with such filth accords with their low-status position at the bottom of the Hindu caste hierarchy, even as their services allow high-status people, such as Brahmans, to maintain their ritual purity.

Members of the Leatherworker (Chamar) caste are ascribed a very low status consonant with their association with the caste occupation of skinning dead animals and tanning the leather. Butchers (Khatiks, in Hindi), who kill and cut up the bodies of animals, also rank low on the caste hierarchy because of their association with violence and death.

However, castes associated with ruling and warfare—and the killing and deaths of human beings—are typically accorded high rank on the caste hierarchy. In these instances, political power and wealth outrank association with violence as the key determinant of caste rank.

Maintenance of purity is associated with the intake of food and drink, not only in terms of the nature of the food itself, but also in terms of who has prepared it or touched it. This requirement is especially true for Hindus, but other religious groups hold to these principles to varying degrees. Generally, person risks pollution—and lowering his own status—if he accepts beverages or cooked foods from the hands of people of lower caste status than his own. His status will remain intact if he accepts food or beverages from people of higher caste rank. Usually, for an observant Hindu of any but the very lowest castes to accept cooked food from a Muslim or Christian is regarded as highly polluting.

In a clear example of pollution associated with dining, a Brahman who consumed a drink of water and a meal of wheat bread with boiled vegetables from the hands of a Sweeper would immediately become polluted and could expect social rejection by his caste fellows. From that moment, fellow Brahmans following traditional pollution rules would refuse food touched by him and would abstain from the usual social interaction with him. He would not be welcome inside Brahman homes—most especially in the ritually pure kitchens—nor would he or his close relatives be considered eligible marriage partners for other Brahmans.

Generally, the acceptance of water and ordinary foods cooked in water from members of lower-ranking castes incurs the greatest pollution. In North India, such foods are known as *kaccha khana,* as contrasted with fine foods cooked in butter or oils, which are known as *pakka khana* . Fine foods can be accepted from members of a few castes slightly lower than one's own. Local hierarchies differ on the specific details of these rules.

Completely raw foods, such as uncooked grains, fresh unpeeled bananas, mangoes, and uncooked vegetables can be accepted by anyone from anyone else, regardless of relative status. Toasted or parched foods, such as roasted peanuts, can also be accepted from anyone without ritual or social repercussions. (Thus, a Brahman may accept gifts of grain from lower-caste patrons for eventual preparation by members of his own caste, or he may purchase and consume roasted peanuts or tangerines from street vendors of unknown caste without worry.)

Water served from an earthen pot may be accepted only from the hands of someone of higher or equal caste ranking, but water served from a brass pot may be accepted even from someone slightly lower on the caste scale. Exceptions to this rule are members of the Water bearer (Bhoi, in Hindi) caste, who are employed to carry water from wells to the homes of the prosperous and from whose hands members of all castes may drink water without becoming polluted, even though Water bearers are not ranked high on the caste scale.

These and a great many other traditional rules pertaining to purity and pollution constantly impinge upon interaction between people of different castes and ranks in India. Although to the non-Indian these rules may seem irrational and bizarre, to most of the people of India they are a ubiquitous and accepted part of life. Thinking about and following purity and pollution rules make it necessary for people to be constantly aware of differences in status. With every drink of water, with every meal, and with every contact with another person, people must ratify the social hierarchy of which they are a part and within which their every act is carried out. The fact that expressions of social status are intricately bound up with events that happen to everyone every day—eating, drinking, bathing, touching, talking—and that transgressions of these rules, whether deliberate or accidental, are seen as having immediately polluting effects on the person of the transgressor, means that every ordinary act of human life serves as a constant reminder of the importance of hierarchy in Indian society.

There are many Indians, particularly among the educated urban elite, who do not follow traditional purity and pollution practices. Dining in each others' homes and in restaurants is common among well-educated people of diverse backgrounds, particularly when they belong to the same economic class. For these people, guarding the family's earthen water pot from inadvertent touch by a low-ranking servant is not the concern as it for a more traditional villager. However, even among those people whose works and actions denigrate traditional purity rules, there is often a reluctance to completely abolish consciousness of purity and pollution from their thinking. It is surely rare for a Sweeper, however well-educated, to invite a Brahman to dinner in his home and have his invitation unself consciously accepted. It is less rare, however, for educated urban colleagues of vastly different caste and religious heritage to enjoy a cup of tea together. Some high caste liberals pride themselves on being free of "casteism" and seek to accept food from the hands of very low-caste people, or even deliberately set out to marry someone from a significantly lower caste or a different religion. Thus, even as they deny it, these progressives affirm the continuing significance of traditional rules of purity, pollution, and hierarchy in Indian society.

SOCIAL INTERDEPENDENCE

One of the great themes pervading Indian life is social interdependence. People are born into groups—families, clans, sub-castes, castes, and religious communities—and live with a constant sense of being part of and inseparable from these groups. A corollary is the notion that everything a person does properly involves interaction with other people. A person's greatest dread, perhaps, is the possibility of being left alone, without social support, to face the necessary challenges of life. This sense of interdependence is extended into the theological realm: the very shape of a person's life is seen as being greatly influenced by divine beings with whom an ongoing relationship must be maintained.

Social interaction is regarded as being of the highest priority, and social bonds are expected to be long lasting. Even economic activities that might in Western culture involve impersonal interactions are in India deeply embedded in a social nexus. All social interaction involves constant attention to hierarchy, respect, honour, the feelings of others, rights and obligations, hospitality, and gifts of food, clothing, and other desirable items. Finely tuned rules of etiquette help facilitate each individual's many social relationships.

Western visitors to India are sometimes startled to find that important government and business officials have left their posts—often for many days at a time—to attend a cousin's wedding or participate in religious activities in a distant part of the country. "He is out of station and will be back in a week or two," the absent official's officemates blandly explain to the frustrated visitor. What is going on is not laziness or hedonistic recreation, but is the official's proper recognition of his need to continually maintain his social ties with relatives, caste fellows, other associates, and God. Without being enmeshed in such ties throughout life, a person cannot hope to maintain long-term efficacy in either economic or social endeavours. Social bonds with relatives must be reinforced at family events or at rites crucial to the religious community. If this is not done, people who could offer vital support in many phases of life would be alienated.

In every activity, there is an assumption that social ties can help a person and that their absence can bring failure. Seldom do people carry out even the simplest task on their own. From birth onward, a child learns that his "fate" has been "written" by divine forces and that his life will be shaped by a plan decided by more powerful beings. When a small child eats, his mother puts the mouthfuls of food into his mouth with her own hand. When a boy climbs a tree to pluck mangoes, another stands below with a basket to receive them. When a girl fetches water from the well in pots on her head, someone at her home helps her unload the pots. When a farmer stacks sheaves of grain onto his bullock cart, he stands atop the cart, catching the sheaves tossed up to him by his son.

A student applying to a college hopes that he has an influential relative or family friend who can put in a good word for him with the director of admissions. At the age of marriage, a young person expects that parents will take care of finding the appropriate bride or groom and arranging all the formalities. At the birth of a child, the new mother is assured that the child's kin will help her attend to the infant's needs. A businessman seeking to arrange a contract relies not only on his own abilities but also on the assistance of well-connected friends and relatives to help finalize the deal. And finally, when facing death, a person is confident that offspring and other relatives will carry out the appropriate funeral rites, including a commemorative feast when, through gifts of clothing and food, continuing social ties are reaffirmed by all in attendance.

LIFE PASSAGES

In India, the ideal stages of life have been most clearly articulated by Hindus. The ancient Hindu ideal rests on childhood, followed by four stages: undergoing religious initiation and becoming a celibate student of religious texts, getting married and becoming a householder, leaving home to become a forest hermit after becoming a grandparent, and becoming a homeless wanderer free of desire for all material things. Although few actually follow this scheme, it serves as a guide for those attempting to live according to valued standards. For Hindus, dharma (a divinely ordained code of proper conduct), karma (the sum of one's deeds in this life and in past lives), and *kismat* (fate) are considered relevant to the course of life (see: The Roots of Indian Religion, ch. 3). Crucial transitions from one phase of life to another are marked by sometimes elaborate rites of passage.

CHILDREN AND CHILDHOOD

Throughout much of India, a baby's birth is celebrated with rites of welcome and blessing—songs, drums, happy distribution of sweets, auspicious unguents, gifts for infant and mother, preparation of horoscopes, and inscriptions in the genealogist's record books. In general, children are deeply desired and welcomed, their presence regarded as a blessing on the household. Babies are often treated like small deities, pampered and cuddled, adorned with makeup and trinkets, and carried about and fed with the finest foods available to the family. Young girls are worshiped as personifications of Hindu goddesses, and little boys are adulated as scions of the clan.

In their children, parents see the future of the lineage and wider kin group, helpers in daily tasks, and providers of security in the parents' old age. These delightful ideals are articulated and enacted over and over again; yet, a coexisting harsher reality emerges from a close examination of events and statistics. Many children lead lives of striking hardship, and many die premature deaths. In general, conditions are significantly worse for girls than for boys.

Birth celebrations for baby daughters are more muted than for sons and are sometimes absent altogether. Although India was once led by a woman prime minister, Indira Gandhi, and Indian women currently hold a wide range of powerful positions in every walk of life, there is a strong cultural bias toward males. Girls are frequently victims of underfeeding, medical neglect, sex-selective abortion, and outright infanticide. According to the 1991 census final population totals, there were 927 females per 1,000 males in India—a figure that has gradually declined from 972 females per 1,000 males in 1901 and from 934 just since 1981.* Much of this imbalance is attained through neglecting the nutritional and health needs of female children, and much is also the result of inadequate health care for women of childbearing years. The sex ratio is even more imbalanced in urban areas (894 per 1,000 in 1991) than in rural areas (938 per 1,000 in 1991), partially because a large number of village men go to work in cities, leaving their wives and children behind in their rural homes.

That girls are victims of fatal neglect and murder has been thoroughly discussed in the Indian press and in scholarly investigations. It has been noted that infant girls are killed with potions of opium in Rajasthan and pastes of poisonous oleander in Tamil Nadu most especially girls preceded by the birth of several sisters. Clinics offering ultrasound and amniocentesis in order to detect and abort female fetuses have become popular in various parts of the country, and many thousands of female foetuses have been so destroyed. In Maharashtra, Rajasthan, and Punjab such selective abortions have been outlawed because of pressure from feminist groups.

---

*Sex ratio has marginally improved to 933 per thousand males according to 2001 census.

More usually, girls are simply fed and cared for less well than their brothers.

The sex ratio is particularly unfavourable to females in the central northern section of the country. For example, according to the 1991 census, in Uttar Pradesh there were 898 females per 1000 males; in Haryana, 861 per 1000; and in Rajasthan 921 per 1000. By contrast, in Kerala, on the southwest coast, a region traditionally noted for matriliny, the sex ratio is reversed, with females outnumbering males 1058 to 1000. In Andhra Pradesh and Tamil Nadu, two large southern states, there are 978 females per 1000 males.

2001 CENSUS (SEX RATIO)

U.P.	898: 1000
Haryana	861: 1000
Rajasthan	921: 1000
Delhi	821: 1000
Kerala	1058: 1000
Tamil Nadu	987: 1000
Andhra Pradesh	978: 1000

Parents favour boys for various reasons. In the north, a boy's value in agricultural endeavours is higher than a girl's, and after marriage a boy continues to live with his parents, ideally supporting them in their old age. Political scientist Philip Oldenburg notes that in some violence-prone regions of the north, having sons may enhance families' capacity to defend themselves and to exercise power. A girl, however, moves away to live with her husband's relatives and with her goes a dowry. Since past few decades the values of dowries have been increasing, and, furthermore, groups that never gave dowries in the past are being pressurized to do so. Thus, a girl child can represent a significant economic liability to her parents. In rice-growing areas, especially in the south, girls receive better treatment, and there is some evidence that the better treatment is related to the value of women as field workers in wet-rice cultivation. Throughout most of India, for Hindus it is important to have a son conduct funeral rites for his parents; a daughter, as a member of her husband's lineage, has not traditionally been able to do so.

For both boys and girls, infant mortality rates tend to be high, and in the absence of confidence that their infants will live, parents tend to produce numerous offspring in the hope that at least two sons will survive to adulthood. Family planning measures are used to a modest degree in India; perhaps 37.5 per cent of couples use contraceptives at least occasionally. Abortion is legal, condoms are advertised on colourful billboards, and government health services offer small bounties for patients undergoing vasectomies and tuballigations. In some regions, most notably Kerala, better health care and higher infant survival rates are associated with lowered fertility rates.

Most children survive infancy and do not fall victim to the cultural and economic pressures alluded to above. The majority of children grow up as valued members of a family, treasured by their parents and encouraged to participate in appropriate activities. Although relative ages of children are always known and reflected in linguistic and deference behavior, there is little age-grading in daily life. Children of all ages associate with each other and with adults, unlike the situation in the West, where age-grading is common.

Studies of Indian psychology by Sudhir Kakar, Alan Roland, and others stress that the young Indian child grows up in intimate emotional contact with the mother and other mothering persons. Because conjugal marital relationships are deemphasized in the joint household, a woman looks to her children to satisfy some of her intimacy needs. Her bond to her children, especially her sons but also her daughters, becomes enormously strong and lasting. A child is suckled on demand, sometimes for years, sleeps with a parent or grandparent, is bathed by doting relatives, and is rarely left alone. Massaged with oil, carried about, gently toilet-trained, and gratified with treats, the young child develops an inner core of well-being and a profound sense of expectation of protection from others. Such indulgent and close relationships produce a symbiotic mode of relating to others and effect the development of a person with a deeply held sense of involvement with relatives, so vital to the Indian family situation.

The young child learns early about hierarchy within the family, as he watches affectionate and respectful relationships between seniors and juniors, males and females. A young child is often carried about by an older sibling, and strong and close sibling bonds usually develop. Bickering among siblings is not as common as it is in the West; rather, most siblings learn to think of themselves as part of a family unit that must work together as it meets the challenges of the outside world.

Young children are encouraged to participate in the numerous rituals that emphasize family ties. The power of sibling relationships is recognized, for example, when a brother touches his sister's feet, honouring in her the principle of feminine divinity, which, if treated appropriately, can bring him prosperity. In calendrical and life-cycle rituals in both the north and the south, sisters bless their brothers and also symbolically request their protection throughout life.

After about four or five years of indulgence, children typically experience greater demands from family members. In villages, children learn the rudiments of agricultural labour, and young children often help with weeding, harvesting, threshing, and the like. Girls learn domestic chores, and boys are encouraged to take cattle for grazing, learn ploughing, and begin to drive bullock carts and ride bicycles. City children also learn household duties, and children of poor families often work as servants in the homes of the prosperous. Some even pick through garbage piles to find shreds of food and fuel.

In some areas, children work as exploited labourers in factories, where they weave carpets for the export market and make matches, glass bangles, and other products. At Sivakasi, in Tamil Nadu, some 45,000 children work in the match, fireworks, and printing industries, comprising perhaps the largest single concentration of child labour in the world. Children reportedly as young as four years old work long hours each day.

Education in a school setting is available for most of India's children, and many young people attend school. Officials state that education is "compulsory," but the reality is that a significant percentage of children—especially girls—fail to become literate and instead carry out many other tasks in order to contribute to family income. More than half of India's children between the ages of six and fourteen—82.2 million—are not in school. Instead they participate in the labour force, even as more privileged children study at government and private schools and prepare for more prestigious jobs. Thus children learn early the realities of socio-economic and urban-rural differentiation and grow up to perpetuate India's hierarchical society.

For many children, especially boys, an important event of young adolescence is religious initiation. Initiation rituals vary among different regions, religious communities, and castes. In the north, girls reach puberty without public notice and in an atmosphere of shyness, whereas in much of the south, puberty celebrations joyously announce to the family and community that a young girl has grown to maturity.

CASTE AND POLITICS

Caste has always played a predominant role in India society during the various stages of history. The British, in particular, to divide the Indians played communal card and encouraged the communal forces in the country through various provisions like special safeguards, protectional special electorates. The policy of 'divide and rule' was aimed at favouring the Muslim League against the Indian National Congress. The 'two nation' theory which was popularized by them ultimately was responsible for the division of India.

Caste is a unique feature for the Indian society and constitutes a well-organized homogeneous and articulate social group. Prof. Rudolph in this concern says, "Within the new context of political democracy caste remains a central element of India's society even while adopting itself to the values and methods of democratic politics. Indeed, it has become one of the chief means by which the Indian mass has been attached to the process of democratic politics."

Mentioning about the complex interplay between caste and politics, Prof. Moriss Jones comments, "Politics is more important to castes and castes are more important to politics than before."

Rajni Kothari has pointed out three aspects of interaction of caste with politics:

(i) Caste is a stratification system in which distances are rigidly maintained through endogamy, pollution and the legitimacy of rituals. Caste as a system of conflict and interaction has received sparse attention. Yet, the fact remains that functionalism and caste cleavages, patterns of alignment and realignment among the various strata, and a continuous striving for social mobility have always been prominent feature for the caste system.

(ii) Secondly, the caste system determines the individuals' social station on the basis of the group to which he is born but also differentiates and assign occupational and economic roles. It, thus, gives a place to every individual from the highest to the lowest and makes for a high degree of identification and integration.

(iii) Thirdly, caste enters the politics through the 'consciousness aspects' highlighted by its symbolism and value structure. This is where the symbolic gestures for cultural mobility such as 'sanskritisation', 'westernization' and 'secularization' assume political overtones in their manifestation. So, according to Rajni Kothari, "it is not politics that gets caste-ridden, it is caste that gets politicized."

The caste groups when they become politically united, become a political force. Due to the introduction of representative democracy based on the principle of universal adult franchise, the numerically strong caste groups have become conscious about their bargaining power. In the democratic set-up, where every vote counts, the numerical preponderance of a caste group gains an additional significance. Caste politics is now closely related to pressure groups and party politics. The voting pattern is based upon, caste based loyalties. 'Caste-alliances' or 'caste appeals' by the politicians is a common occurrence. In the selection of the candidates for a constituency, the deciding factor is whether he can get the support of a particular caste or castes. For example, the selection of candidates and their election in Haryana is highly influenced by the Jats and the Ahirs, in Rajasthan by Rajputs and Jats, in Karnataka by the Vokkalinga and the Lingayat, etc. This has encouraged caste wars and social tensions. The non-privileged caste groups have become organized and assertive for their rights.

Caste has emerged as a major tool for the management of power. The distribution of power is done according to dominance and awareness of the caste groups. It is further enhanced by the reservation policy which is bringing gradual social change in the social set-up. The high caste monopoly is being broken by the Constitutional gurantees to the perceived lower castes in the form of 'reservations'. The Constitutional provisions for special reservations for the Scheduled Castes, the scheduled tubes and other backward tribes has brought new awareness among the people.

The champions of caste politics argue that it is due to social and economic backwardness which these castes historically suffered that warrants reservations. Pradipta Chaudhary in the *Indian Express* (29 May, 2006) comments, "Caste is being used as the sole criteria in public policy oriented towards positive discrimination." The quotas specified by the government are 15 per cent for the Scheduled Castes, 7.5 per cent for the Scheduled Tribes and 27 per cent for the OBC.

Recently, the government decided to introduce the 27 per cent OBC quote in the higher education sector both public and private which created a lot of controversy. The quota would apply to the elite governmental institutions, including the IITs, IIMs, medical college, etc. and a dozen more institutions including that receive no government aid, under the pretext that new States as deemed universities—a status that UGC confers and hence, these come in purview of direct governmental interference.

So Prof. Srinivas has aptly said, that caste "is so tacitly and so completely accepted by all, including most vocal elements in condemning it, that it is everywhere the unit of social action."

CHAPTER 2

Historical Perspective of Reservation

India is a country with highly rigid caste-based hierarchical structure and has ascending order of privileges and descending order of disabilities.

In India, reservation is a policy by which a fixed number of slots in governmental and educational institutionally are allotted to members of certain communities based on criteria like castes, class etc. The overwhelming majority in the nation that is still backward-socially, economically, educationally and politically are eligible for reservations. The victims of entrenched backwardness comprise the Scheduled Castes (SCs), Scheduled Tribes (STs) and Other Backward Classes (OBCs).

Reservation is taken as a variety of measure designed to end the oppressive discrimination and remedy the related in justice they had suffered over the centuries. The socially and educationally backward classes of citizens, such as the Scheduled Castes and Scheduled Tribes have been subjected to discrimination and deprivation for thousands of years, hence reservations are an instrument for the advancement of the socially and educationally backward classes.

India is a Parliamentary Democracy, wedded to the ideal of preserving civil liberties and individual rights. India is making an attempt to address the needs of the under represented sections of the society, to assume equality of opportunity to them and to end discrimination against members of groups that have been historically exposed to discrimination.

The nature and concept of reservations is a vast and controversial one. Even in terms of a historical account of reservations in India, it would be impossible to cover most of its aspects. In this chapter, therefore, we shall examine in brief some of the key issues and some of the more significant historical and legal moments concerning the development of a reservations policy in India, all of which require much more attention and analysis. A great deal has been written against reservations policies since the acceptance of the Mandal Commission Report in 1991 in favour of reservations in higher education and government services for the Other Backward Classes of India. Very little has been written by the beneficiaries of reservations, whether in book form or in the form of articles in the national press. Those who are vociferous and loud in their criticism of reservations invariably belong to the dominant groups, who have been enjoying the benefits of, if not a monopoly over, education, wealth, land and public services.

On the other hand, the worst victims of the condemnation, persecution and exploitation of contemporary society have been the shudras, dalits (untouchables, unseeables and unapproachables) and women. There are many scholars and intellectuals in India whose vision get easily stigmatised by phrases and slogans borrowed from the west and other lands. Writers belonging to the Hindu upper castes - not Muslims, Christians or Buddhists - have often asserted that it was the British who introduced the policy of 'Divide and Rule' into India. The phrase 'divide and rule' was infact originally deployed by the dominating classes of Rome who conquered a large portion of the world and had to devise ways and means to maintain their empire and supremacy. But if we seriously and earnestly study the history of man, the principle of divide and rule was really devised by the Brahmans in India who framed laws and rules in the name of Dharma and Brahma to divide society vertically and horizontally and exploit large numbers of people—poor, deprived, ignorant and divided - so that a few on top may continue to enjoy the good things of life —power, prestige, privileges and so on. Reservations were not introduced, as some Hindu writers have asserted, so that the British could 'divide and rule' Indians. The reservation or quota system was introduced in Malta before it was even mentioned in India. Yugoslavia had five nationalities and six linguistic groups.

Power had to be shared and a kind of, quota system was established to keep the country united. Americans, whether they agree or not, were influenced by the Indian experiment and 'affirmative action' was introduced in the 1960s with a view to giving a share to the discrimination - African-Americans, Native Americans and other ethnic minorities. Other countries of Europe and America including Great Britain are now thinking along the lines of some reservation or affirmative action for ethnic and other minorities who are victims of discrimination by the dominating groups.

RESERVATION: A BRIEF HISTORY

India is a divided into many castes or subcastes, as a result of social hierarchy called the caste system being practiced. The age old traditional caste system which is very oppressive, led to segregation of the lower castes and put many prohibitions including educational and denied various rights to them. The discrimination in the Indian society was further augumented by the policies of British in India.

British India was facing problems right from the 18th century when Lord Cornwallis took over as governor general in 1786. The East India Company was reeking with corruption. Administrators often find scapegoats and Cornwallis was no exception. He blamed the Indians for maladministration and inefficiency which resulted in large losses of revenue. Cornwallis introduced certain reforms and closed the doors to employment for the Indians, except in the lower ranks of administration. Scions of the upper castes and affluent families turned to other professions, especially the profession of law. Another event which affected Indians in the services was the introduction of English as the official language by Lord Macaulay. It was decided in the Council with Lord Macaulay as law minister that while Madrassas and Sanskrit schools would be allowed to function, official business was to be conducted in English. "The cause of English was still further advanced by the regulation introduced by the first Lord Hardinge that all public services were to be filled by an open competition examination held by the Council (the successor of the Committee of Public Instruction), preference being given to the knowledge of English. Virtually, English education was made the only passport to higher appointments available to the Indians, and hence its popularity and rapid progress were equally assured" (Mazumdar, *An Advanced History of India:818).* While the benefits of English education were reaped by members of affluent and newly emerging middle class people, the masses remained ignorant and backward.

Brahmans in the Madras presidency and the Bhadralok in the Bengal presidency took advantage of the new educational policy and the central place of the English language within it and occupied most of the posts available in the administration.

The policy of reservations took shape take nineteenth and early twentieth centuries. The development of organized movements, especially in Southern India, could be considered its starting point. It was an attempt to curtail the power of Brahmans, who constituted only about 3 per cent of the population in these areas, and yet, dominated the elite positions in the civil services and such related professions that were open to all Indian under the British rule. The inequalities in the society were perpetuated by Brahmans in India, who in the name of 'Dharma' framed such laws, rules and regulations which attempted to divide society vertically and horizontally both, and exploit ignorant, poor and deprived masses of people. They also attempted to maintain their status quo and enjoy the power, prestige and privileges, so long enjoyed by them.

This wave of anti-Brahman movements put an immense pressure to reserve seats for non-Brahman in the public service and also to give aid to the non-Brahmans in educational institutions. However, according to a few writers, reservations were introduced by British so that they could 'divide and rule' Indians. In the Indian context, reservations were introduced during the last decades of the 19th century at a time when the subcontinent could be broadly divided according to two main forms of governance—British India and the 600 princely states. Some of these princely states were progressive and eager to modernise through the promotion of education and industry; and by maintaining unity among their own people. Mysore in south India and Baroda and Kolhapur in western India took considerable interest in the awakening and advancement of the minorities and deprived sections of society.

The Backward Classes Movement began in Madras in 1916 in the form of Non-Brahman conference, organized by the leaders of what later came to be known as the Justice party, representing different parts of the multilingual presidency of Madras. This movement had the objective of displacing Brahmans, who were in minority and yet dominated higher education, the professions and the bureaucracy. This movement united various castes, ethnic and religious groups in the presidency is opposition to the Brahmans.

The pressure for non-Brahman reservation was being introduced in the Princely state of Mysore, Bombay and Madras presidencies in the 1920s, Kannadiga Brahmans also had a very small share in public services. In the princely state of Mysore, the Tamil Brahmans enjoyed monopoly over all the jobs. The Mysore Government in 1921 introduced reservations in the public service positions and higher educational admission, especially to provide a larger share to the caste and communities who had little share in the administration viz. the Kannadiga Brahmans, Vokkalligas and Lingayats beside the

Muslims and the untouchable castes. Reservations were, thus, introduced in favour of a number of castes and communities that had little share in administration.

In the year 1925, similar reservations were introduced in Bombay. Little later, in Madras, an attempt was made to substantially represent non-Brahman communities in the new public service appointments. In 1926, according to specific quotas introduced in the public appointments, every fifteen appointments would be allocated in such a way that two appointments are for Brahmans. Two for 'Backward' or low-caste Hindus, six to other Hindus, six to other Hindus, two to depressed classes or untouchables, two to Anglo-Indians and Christians and one to Muslim.

By the year 1930s, reservation policies began to be implemented throughout India. As the largest religious minority, Muslims shared a major complaint that they had a very little share in administration. The upper caste Hindus were making use of the educational facilities provided by British and Christian Missionaries, while Muslims due to regional sentiments had decided not to learn English, which was considered as language of infidels by them. As a result, the upper caste Hindus enjoyed a large share in the bureaucracy. Under the leadership of Agha Khan, leader of the Ismaili sect, a delegation of Muslim Nawabs, Landlords and prominent persons presented a memorandum demanding a share in administration in proportion to their population which was positively considered by the Viceory. In 1909, the Morley Minto Reforms introduced communal electoral, by reserving seats to Indian Muslims in the Legislations but now for the lower castes. Various provisions were made in the Government of India Act of 1919 granting the Muslims due share and other facilities.

In 1927, the Simon Commission, recommended the reservations of seats for the lower castes in the Legislative Council, in order to increase their politics of representation. Although this implementation was considered as temporary, to improve the conditions of the lower castes, which would later make reservation unnecessary.

The untouchables or the 'depressed classes' had joined the Army in the Presidencies and fought battles for the British Empire. While in the army, the untouchable soldiers got educated and learnt a lot from the new ideas. The untouchables also produced various other jobs under the British. They worked as cooks, sweepers, butlers, gardeners, ayahs etc. with the British families. But, the Brahminisation of the Bengal Army led to reduction of soldiers of untouchable origin in the Bengal Army and also resulted in Mutiny. However they continued to be enlisted in the presidency armies of Bombay and Madras.

The British changed their recruitment policies according to their political needs. Christian missionaries contributed a great deal towards awakening the untouchables and promoting literacy, in spite of discouragement by the British officers, many of whom thought that missionary work was a nuisance.

The untouchables, still continued to be politically, not imparted as mentioned by Ibbetson, the famous census Commissioner, they had not organized themselves as a political force and were merely satisfied with minor concessions and facilities which could uplift them. It was only Dr. B.R. Ambedkar, the leader of India's untouchables who ardently advocated separate electorate and seats for the untouchable community.

Mahatma Gandhi was totally opposed to this separation of the 'Harijans' or 'the people of God' or untouchables from the rest of the community. Yet, much to reluctance of Mahatma Gandhi, the British had established separate electorates and seats for four of India's minority communities namely, Muslims, Christians, Sikhs and Anglo Indians. In 1932, the British Government introduced the Communal Award by which "the Depressed Classes are granted separate seats in the Provincial Assemblies and the right of double vote under which they were to elect their own representatives and to vote also in the general constituencies." These constitutional proposals, which included provisions of separate electorates for the 'depressed classes' in untouchables was disliked by Mahatma Gandhi believing the untouchables are part and parcel of the Hindu Community, threatened to go on fast into death. Dr. Ambedkar, agreed to abandon separate communal electorate and an agreement was signed to save the life of Mahatma Gandhi which abandoned separate communal electorate but demanded a number of seats to be reserved for them within the allotment of seats to the Hindu Community, to safeguard the interest of untouchables. The agreement is known as the Poona Pact, 1932 and its provisions were as follows:

(1) There shall be seats reserved for the depressed classes out of the general electorate seats in the Provisional Legislatures. A total of 148 seats were reserved for them i.e. from Madras 30 seats, Bombay with Sind 15 seats, Punjab 8 seats, Bihar and Orissa 18 seats, Central Provinces 20 seats, Assam 7 seats, Bengal 30 seats and United Provinces 20 seats would be reserved.

(2) Election to these seats shall be by joint electorate, subject to the following procedures: All members of the depressed classes, registered in the general electoral roll in a constituency will form an electoral college, which will elect a panel of four candidates belonging to the depressed classes for each such reserved seat, by the method of the single vote; the four persons getting the highest number of votes in such primary election shall be candidates for election by the general electorate.

(3) Representation of the depressed classes in the central legislature shall likewise be on the principle of joint electorates and reserved seats by the method of primary elections in the manner prescribed for in Clause 2 above, for their representation in the provincial legislature. As regards the share in the administration, the following provisions were made in the Poona Pact:

There shall be no disabilities attached to any one on the ground of his being a member of the depressed classes in regard to any election to local bodies, or appointment to the public services. Every endeavour shall be made to secure fair representation of the depressed classes in these respects subject to such educational qualifications as may be laid down for appointment to the public services. As against the 78 seats allotted to the depressed classes in the state legislature, the Poona Pact gave 148 seats. However, untouchables lost the right to elect their own representatives and this right was transferred to the Hindus. As a result, the elected members remained faithful to the parties and their leaders who funded their elections.

The Poona Pact had deep impact and also served as a hindrance in their progress in other fields also. The government issued orders regarding reservation in services on July 7, 1934.

This compromise was further continued in the Government of India Act of 1935, which established a system of reserved seats, not separate electorate for two communities i.e. the untouchables and the tribals officially called as the 'Scheduled Castes' (SCs) and the 'Scheduled Tribes' (STs). Infact, this act had introduced the term of Scheduled Castes, which was then a list of castes, races and tribes which were considered as lower castes.

In order to implement the provisions of the Government of India Act of 1935, the list of officially Scheduled Castes and Scheduled Tribes was drawn in 1936, based on the information collected in 1931 census of India about ethnic or caste status of the people and also disadvantages associated with different ethnic and caste communities. "In principle, SCs were to be identified as communities that were backward because of untouchability, defined essentially in terms of their ritually 'polluting' status in the Hindu society. There was also an admixture of economic and educational criteria, as well as some considerations of local politics, and it was generally the socio-economically lowest group of Hindus in any given area who were ultimately included in the SC list. The designation of STs was less problematic, spatial and cultural isolation was the key and these characteristics were closely correlated with socio-economic backwardness. The 1936 list of SCs and STs were largely duplicated in independent India, with some minor additions (e.g. to include and few 'backward' Sikh and neo-Buddhist castes) in the early 1950s and at several times thereafter.

The Indian provincial governments that were constituted in 1937, not only maintained, but also expanded previously enacted reservations in public service jobs and educational admissions for religious minority groups and for the depressed classes. At the federal level, reservations were adopted only in public services and only for the religious minorities.

Dr. B.R. Ambedkar laid the foundations of All India Depressed Classes Federation to support the improvement of the Scheduled Castes, in 1942. He was appointed as member of the Viceroy's Executive Council and submitted a memorandum "On the grievances of the Scheduled Castes" elucidating their grievances and demanded reservations for the Scheduled Castes in public services, scholarships and stipends for education within the country and abroad. The recommendations were duly accepted by the Viceroy and referred to the Secretary of State, who accepted the recommendations. As a result, for the first time in the history, in 1942, the Scheduled Castes were allowed 8.5 per cent reservations in civil services and other facilities as well.

After India achieved independence in 1947, drafting Committee with Ambedkar as Chairman was constituted to draft the Constitution of India. A few members of the Constituent Assembly were opposed to the provisions of reservations in favour of the depressed classes. The Constitution of India, included safeguards for the depressed and Other Backward Classes.

The Constitution of India came into force from 26 January, 1950. The Constitution prohibits any discrimination based on religion, race, caste, sex and place of birth. Even while providing equality of opportunity to ensure reservations, 'for the advancement of any socially and educationally backward classes of citizens or for the Scheduled Castes and the Scheduled Tribes'. "The provisions for reservations of seats in the state legislature initially was made for a period of 10 years ending in 1960. This has recently been extended up to 2010. Provision was also made for reservation in public services, which has no time limit. Surprisingly, prime ministers, political leaders and journalists have been making speeches and writing articles giving the impression that it is reservations in public services which have been extended for ten years. Reservations made under Article 335 read together with Article 46 has no time limit prescribed under the Constitution. Reservation was also made in favour of Anglo Indians for a shorter period in view of the difficulties and disabilities peculiar to them.

CONSTITUTIONAL PROVISIONS

The principle of equality is an important feature of the Constitution of India. The state is to treat all citizens equally, irrespective of their caste, race, religion, sex, descent, place of birth, residence and so on, and no citizen would be discriminated against by the State only on any of these grounds. However, the exceptions in this regard, can be made in favour of women, children, Other Backward Classes, the Scheduled Castes, the Scheduled Tribes and the weaker sections of the people.

Article 14 guarantees equality to all and mentions, 'The State shall not deny to any person equality before the law or the equal protection of the laws within the territory of India.

Article 15(1) of the Constitution prohibits discrimination on the grounds of religion, race, caste, sex or place of birth. Article 15(2) guarantees equal access for everyone to public facilities like wells, restaurants etc. However, under Article 15(3), any special provision may be made for women and children in general and belonging to all social groups transcending the castes, religion etc. for their advancement and welfare in all the fields. Under Article 15(4), special provisions, may be made for the advancement of any socially and educationally backward classes and for the Scheduled Castes and the Scheduled Tribes. This sub-clause was inserted by an amendment in 1951, ending the ambivalence about the positive discrimination. The expression "backward class" is interpreted by the Supreme Court as "socially and educationally backwards." Moreover, the Scheduled Castes and the Scheduled Tribes are separated from the expression backward classes there to make a distinction between these and the backward classes. Hence, the popular term, the other Backward Classes' or the OBCs distinguished from the Schedule Castes and the Scheduled Tribes.

Article 16 assures the equality of opportunity in matters of public employment. Article 16(4) permits the state to make any provision for the reservation of appointments or posts in favour of any backward class, which in the opinion of the state is not adequately represented in the services under the state. Article 16(4) permits the state to make any provision for the reservation of appointments or posts in favour of any backward classes, which in the opinion of the state is not adequately represented in the services under the State. The Supreme Court in its decisions on the reservations has interpreted the expression 'backward classes' in Article 16(4) to mean 'socially and educationally backward, 'although Article 16(4) merely refers to the 'backward classes'. The court has explicitly rejected 'economic backwardness' as the only criterion for the reservations under Article 16(4) and stated that the economic backwardness has to be on account of the social and the educational backwardness."

Article 46 mentions 'weaker sections' whose 'economic interests as well as educational interests have to be taken into consideration with special care, protecting them from all forms of 'social injustice and exploitation'. Article 46 of the Constitution incorporating the Directive Principles of State Policy says, "The State shall promote with special care the educational and economic interests of the weaker sections of the people, and in particular, of the Scheduled Castes and the

Scheduled Tribes, and shall protect them from social injustice and all forms of exploitation." This article also supplements the view that weaker sections are other section other than the Scheduled Castes and Scheduled Tribes, are backward both socially and educationally, and need to be protected from social injustice and all forms of exploitation. However, merely the economically weak or backward section would not qualify for promotion of their interests under this article.

Who is a member of the Scheduled Castes and the Scheduled Tribes has been defined under Article 366 of the Constitution. Article 366, section 24 states that 'Scheduled Castes' means such castes, race or tribes or parts of or groups in such castes, race, tribes as are deemed under Article 341 to be Scheduled Castes for the purposes of the Constitution, Article 366, section 25 means such tribes or tribal communities or parts or groups within such tribal communities as are deemed under Article 342 to be the Scheduled Tribes for the purposes of the Constitution. Initially, only the members of the Scheduled Castes professing Hinduism and four castes among the Sikhs (Kabir panthis, Ramdassias, Sikhigars and Muzhbis) were included which was later in 1956 extended to include all Scheduled Castes professing Sikhism. Meanwhile in October 1956, Ambedkar revived Buddhism and started mass conversion into Buddhism. The Government of India, however, issued orders to the effect that they are ineligible to any of the concessions admissible to Scheduled Castes. In 1990, the Scheduled Castes who were professing Buddhism were also included among the Scheduled Castes. The Scheduled Tribes have no such restrictions and Animists, Hindus, Christians or Buddhists, the category of Other Backward Classes was evolved by the depressed classes and Aboriginal Tribes Committee constituted by the Government of Bombay whose report was published duly in 1930. Almost 125 castes were incorporated in the OBC list in 1930. Later a list of 228 Intermediate communities were declared in 1942 mainly for the purposes of recruitment to government service consisting of peasant and artisan communities the Indian Christian and the Muslims which was later cancelled.

So, in the political arena, the Constitution framers were not supportive of the idea that the religious minority communities deserved any kind of special status, yet they retained the stream of the reserved seats for the Scheduled Castes and the Scheduled Tribes, which had been first introduced by the Government of India Act of 1935. According to Articles 330, 332 and 334 of the Constitution, a certain number of parliamentary constituencies, both at the national and state level, has to be represented by a scheduled caste member, with the members of reserved seats proportional to the scheduled population in the constituency, and same for the scheduled tribe member. Although Article 331, limits the period of such reservations by twenty years the reservations have been regularly extended by amendment for additional period of ten years.

In the sphere of employment, the Constitution is against any discrimination in the public employment, which is supplemented with section 4 of the Article 16, which permits the state to make, "any provision for the reservation of appointments or posts in favour of any backward class of citizen, which, in the opinion of the state is not adequately represented in the service under the state." Along with this, Article 335 asserts that the claims of the Scheduled castes and the Scheduled tribes shall be taken into consideration, consistent with the maintenance of efficiency of administration, and it instructs the Central Government to a certain percentage of jobs for the Scheduled Castes and the Scheduled Tribes in civil and technical services, in state run and semi-autonomous enterprises, and in private as well as public technical institutions.

In the sphere of education, originally the Constitution banned any kind of discrimination in the government aided educational institutions as mentioned in Article 29, section 2.

Hence, in the independent India since 1950, there has been a clear constitutional basis for positive discrimination in favour of backward groups, which includes "the Scheduled Castes and the Scheduled Tribes explicitly and the weaker section or the backward classes" potentially. The reserved seats for the Scheduled Castes and the Scheduled Tribes in the elected legislative bodies of the century are well accepted and have become more or less become permanent feature, while reservations in the fields of employment and education are encouraged. The contentious issues are not so much rising out of the Scheduled Castes and the Scheduled Tribes reservations, but from the efforts to expand the range of reservations granted to "Other Backward Classes" (OBCs). The ruling Congress party had earlier rejected the national reservations for the OBCs although it found favour of various state governments who favoured reservations to the groups that they deemed 'necessary'. In few parts of southern India, many OBCs were given favours in the shape of positive education in employment and employment.

With the SC and ST reservations going firm ground, many more low and middle castes Hindus started agitation to include them in the category of reservations. But their demands were partially met at the state level by the 1970s, but seriously considered at the national level until the publication of Mandal Commission in the early 1981.

LANDMARK CASES

Post-independence India has witnessed many landmark cases which have affected the administration as well as interests of the Scheduled Castes, Scheduled Tribes and Other Backward Classes.

Article 16(1) guarantees equality of opportunity in matters of public employment etc. Reservations in public services and educational institutions were created with a view to give a share to the members of society who had been denied opportunities in the past. This naturally antagonized those sections of society who had been enjoying the monopoly of power. Immediately after the adoption of the Constitution, the provision of reservation under Article 16 was challenged through a writ petition field in the Madras High Court (*State of Madras* vs. *Champakam Dorairajan, April* 1951). The case came before the Supreme Court of India in which it was held that the communal government order of the Madras government fixing the proportion of students of each community that could be admitted to state educational institutions was *ultra vires* under Article 19(2) which states that no citizen shall be denied admission into any educational institution maintained by or receiving aid from the state on grounds only of religion, race, caste, or language and was not saved by the provisions of Article 16. There was considerable protest in the southern states as the result of which the Constitution was amended for the first time, and Clause 15(4) added:

> Article 15(4) states: nothing in this Article or in Clause (2) of Article 29 shall prevent the state from making any special provision for the advancement of any socially and educationally backward classes of citizens or for the Scheduled Castes and the Scheduled Tribes. Those who are opposed to reservations in public services have challenged all orders issued by the government under Article 15(1) or under Article 16. Article 226 (on the enforcement of fundamental rights by a High Court) are invoked and writ petitions are filed before the High Court. Sometimes the government comes before the Supreme Court, and sometimes it is the petitioners, if they feel aggrieved, who do so. Judicial process had routinely and effectively been used to obstruct the progress or to delay the implementation of reservation orders. In the famous case of *Balaji versus Mysore state in 1962*, reservation orders were challenged on the basis that the lists of backward classes were prepared only on the basis of caste and that this was unconstitutional.

The Supreme Court struck down the Mysore Backward Classes list. In the *Chitralekha case* similar claims were again taken up *Chitralekha vs. State of Mysore, 1964*. The Supreme Court interpreted the Balaji case in a different light. It was pointed out that two principles were prominent from the observations in Balaji's case i.e. (i) 'the caste of a group of citizens may be a relevant circumstance in ascertaining their social backwardness' and (ii) though it is a relevant factor to determine the social backwardness of a class of citizens, 'it cannot be the sole or dominant test'. In another landmark case, namely, *Jayasree versus State of Kerala* (1976), the Supreme Court accepted the logic of the Kerala High Court that economic backwardness plays a part in social and educational backwardness. In the *Thomas case (State of Kerala versus N.H. Thomas, 1976)* the Supreme Court upheld caste based reservation. The Supreme Court also observed that the aim of the Constitution is to eliminate caste from the affairs of the state. Yet, certain backward castes have to be abolished ultimately. The implementation of the recommendations of the Mandal Commission was challenged and opposed not only by angry students belonging to the Hindu upper castes, but also by the Supreme Court Bar association. A writ petition was filed in the name of Indira Sawhney, one of the practising advocates of the Supreme Court. Even though the rights of Scheduled Castes had nothing to do with the subject of the OBCs of the Mandal Commission report, certain items affecting them were included as issues. Justice Ahmedi raised an objection and did not comment on the issues during the proceedings. The promotion of Scheduled Castes was discussed and the Supreme Court held that there should be no reservations in promotion. In spite of all the opposition to Mandal, reservations in favour of the Other Backward Classes to the extent of 27 per cent was upheld and the agitationists were disappointed. Besides these there are landmark cases like the *Rangachari case (Rangachari vs. General Manager, 1962), Devadasan case (Devadasan vs. Union of India, 1964*; which was ruled out in the Indira Sawhney case), *Hira Lal* case, and the recently decided PGIMS Chandigarh Case (reservation in medical colleges) and *Ajit Singh Janjua case (Seniority in Promotion case)* which have adversely affected the interests of the Scheduled Castes and Scheduled Tribes. Reservations were originally provided for the Scheduled Castes and schedules tribes. It was extended to the Other Backward Classes at the national level in 1993. Several states have passed their own laws and granted reservations to backward sections of society.

It was held by the Supreme Court of India that reservations can be made under an executive order.

However, in view of the recent judgements of the Supreme Court affecting the Scheduled Castes which have stirred the minds of the Scheduled Castes and Scheduled Tribes, the government is under pressure to enact a law so that the judiciary may not decide against the deprived and disadvantaged sections of society. Besides the Scheduled Castes, Scheduled Tribes and Other Backward Classes, Christians of dalit origin and backward sections of Muslim society are also staking their claim for a share in governance. After independence and the creation of Pakistan, only a few Muslims have been able to enter public services. There is a genuine need to make provisions in order to make the bureaucracy more representative. Women who comprise about 49-50 per cent of population also deserve consideration for reservation—and not only in the legislature but also in the bureaucracy. The slogans of past viz., 'Religion in danger', 'Dhamma is in danger' or 'Islam is in danger', is not being raised nowadays a new slogan is being raised, "Abolish reservations because merit and efficiency are in danger." This is often heard in the Supreme Court also. Those who are opposing reservations in public services and educational institutions do so because their personal interests are in jeopardy. Those who made the provisions in the Constitution had the interest of the nation in view. If more and more people take part in decision-making—which also means in the execution and implementation of these decisions taken in a democratic manner—the country will benefit. Those who want to maintain the status quo and consider their personal interests above the national interest, oppose reservations. Dominating groups who have been enjoying a monopoly of power are also notorious for corrupt practices. It is a matter of great concern that our country's name appears among the first four most corrupt countries of the world. We hope that this pernicious development also attracts the attention of the people who champion for the rightful cause of merit, so that our country could progress and make a place for itself in the knowledge based economy.

CHAPTER 3

An Alternative Perception of the Minorities

One of the descriptions of the concept of minority is "non-dominant ground," on the basis of which Indian Constitution recognises religious minorities, linguistic minorities, cultural minorities and minorities possessing special scripts of their own.

Dr. Ambedkar had proposed a set of principle justifying preferential treatment for the minorities and also, suggested an entire complex of public institutions and policy measures to combat disadvantages faced by them. He worked on an alternative perception of minority rights.

After the creation of the Constituent Assembly for framing of the future Constitution in India, the working Committee of the All-India Scheduled Caste Federation had asked Dr. Ambedkar to prepare a Memorandum on the safeguards of the Scheduled Castes for being submitted to the Constituent Assembly on behalf of the Federation. He had not mentioned the rights of Dalits but elucidated a deep understanding about the fundamental rights, minority rights and rights of the Scheduled Castes. He was conscious of the fact that there would severe opposition and criticism of his view that the

"Dalits are not minorities." He underscored the difference between minorities and such disadvantaged groups as untouchables in India. Although there is danger of discrimination to minorities, it is qualitatively minor as compared to what the untouchables had to suffer. Also, "Discrimination towards minority is not in terms of number, because of which, they are usually called a minorities."

Ambedkar presented his views on the minority character of the ex-untouchables in the Constituent Assembly Debates in India and said, 'We claim that we must be treated as a distinct minority, separate from the Hindu Community. Our minority character has been hitherto concealed by our inclusion in the Hindu Community, but as a matter of fact there is really no link between the depressed classes and the Hindu community.... The untouchables and touchables may have grown and may form a part of one culture or religion, but, if, therefore, they were to be considered to be parts of the same 'society' then the term 'society' will lose all its meaning and this will give rise to confusion.... They, the caste and the out caste belong to one culture they belong to different societies ... it would be ... foolish to say that because they have grown up as a part of the Hindu culture, the caste and the outcaste make up one society."

Ambedkar explained, "The Dalits are a minority because their social, economic and educational condition is worst than that of the citizens and other minorities in India. He went on to argue that the Dalits need special safeguards against the tyranny and discrimination of the majority. He argued that to state that the Scheduled Castes are not a minority is to misunderstand the meaning of the term "minority." Separation in religion alone is not the only criteria of the minority. Social discrimination constitutes the real test for determining whether a social group is or not a minority. The untouchables have been denied their very personhood and consequently, the basis of their treatment as equal.

Ambedkar's argument is based on history and "he demonstrated the fact that the Dalits are economically dependent upon the caste Hindus. This economic dependence has other consequence. He dies in the condition of poverty and degradation which proceeds from it. The Hindu code of life bestows many privileges on the upper castes while it heaps upon the untouchables with indignities. These have led to untouchables to perpetuate slavery."

Indian society is multi-structured and highly fragmented into religion and caste groups. The hierarchal system prevalent in India, over centuries carries with it, the axis of pollution and purity in one hand, and dominant Hindu religious groups as against the minority religious groups. The Hindu, by virtue of their population which is in majority, control the affairs of Indian social scene largely. Although, the fact remains that there are internal struggle based on caste considerations amongst the Hindus, still they attempt to have a greater share than the lower castes. Due to this social and economic inequalities are created, justified and perpetuated. The caste hierarchical system had dehumanized the lower caste. Social discrimination against the minorities is still prevalent in one form or another and perpetuated by the dominant groups, who try to corner the minority religious groups and make them subjected to inequalities.

Dr. Ambedkar was quite aware of this social situation. He played a crucial role in drawing the attention of the people towards the pitiable social and economic conditions of this large segment of the Indian population and highlighting the need for providing social and economic justice to them. He tried his best to correct the social imbalances to the best of his ability. He had visualized that these religious and caste considerations had worked to the disadvantage of the lower castes, religious and linguistic minorities. He made an dispassionate attempt to analyse the concept of "Minorities" and justified special safeguards for them.

Ambedkar said, "My definition of democracy is a form and method of government whereby revolutionary changes in the economic and social life of the people are brought about without bloodshed." In a true democracy, he wanted that there should be no glaring inequalities in the society and "there must not be an oppressed or suppressed class". In other words, he said, "There must not be a class which has got all the privileges and a class which has got all the burdens to carry, such a thing, such a division, such an organization of society has within itself the germs of bloody revolution and perhaps it would be impossible for the democracy to cure them."

He considered this social democracy would provide lasting solution to emancipation of Dalits as well as of the entire society. He championed that equality of opportunity should be given to all citizens irrespective of their religion, language, etc. The structure of political democracy in independent India opened up new avenues for the assertion and articulation of dalit identity.

MINORITY RIGHTS IN INDIA AND THE MINORITY COMMISSION

The Indian Constitution has not defined the word 'minority'. The word 'minority' implies a group of persons numerically smaller than others. The Encyclopaedia Britannica explains minorities as "groups held together by ties of common descent, language or religious faith and feeling themselves different in those respect from the majority of the inhabitants of a given entity."

The sensitivity for minority rights is a major part of the adoption and establishment of democracy in India. Infact, the Constitution of India accords not only sufficient safeguards to minorities but also deals with the subject matter in minute details than found in any other Constitution. The minority safeguards are entrenched in the Constitution, most of which are fundamental and permanent. The Judiciary in India has been given special responsibility to protect the minority rights. India is a secular state which is impartial towards all religions. It is in the interest of minorities of any form itself that it stands committed to democratic and secular values.

The Judiciary has shown sensitivity towards protecting the rights of minorities as mentioned in the Constitution. Chief Justice, S.R. Das in Kerala Education Bill exhibits sacred commitment for the minority rights when he says, "So long as the Constitution stands as it is and is not altered, it is, we conceive, the duty of this court to uphold the fundamental duty of this court to uphold the fundamental rights and thereby honour the sacred obligation to the minority communities who are our own."

The Supreme Court of India has played an active role in providing constitutional protection to the minority communities. When the linguistic and religious minorities had failed to get protection through the political process, they have resorted to legal process and the Court come to their aid. For this the Court has maintained, "It is well said that in order to treat some persons equally, we must treat them differently. We have to recognize a fair degree of discrimination in favour of minorities." (Justice Shetty in St. Stephens College Case, 1992).

The Constitution of India specifically recognizes religious minorities, linguistic minorities, cultural minorities possessing special scripts of their own, untouchables, socially and educationally backward classes, Scheduled Castes and Scheduled Tribes.

The Constitution of India recognizes eighteen major languages spoken by majority of the people and hundreds of other languages and dialects which are spoken by the people in the rural areas. A major demand of the linguistic minorities has been of the inclusion of their language in the eighth schedule of the Constitution.

The Judiciary has defined that if Constitution in any community which is numerically less than 50 per cent of the population is considered as 'minority group'. Based upon this definition, the Government of India has declared five religious groups as national minorities which are Muslims, Christians, Sikhs, Buddhists and Parsis.

Although Hinduism is the religion of the majority of Indians, Muslims and Sikhs etc. have tried to maintain their group identities while Jains, Buddhists and Christians do not exhibit fundamentalism and have stayed in the mainstream of Indian politics. Moreover, the question of Muslim minority in India remains to be complex and unsolved even today. The BJP, along with its various wings like RSS, BJP, Bajrang Dal, Sadhu Samaj, Dharma Sansad etc. aim at Hinduisation of India and establishment of Hindu Rashtra. Hence, majority communalism has acquired dangerous dimensions.

INDIAN CONSTITUTION AND THE MINORITY RIGHTS

The Constitution of India does not give minorities any special rights, the same rights are given to majority as well. The Constitution offers only a few safeguards to the rights of the minorities through Articles 29 and 30.

The Constitution approaches the issue of protecting the minorities by two methods, (i) The guarantee of what might be considered as a negative quality, which protected them from the possibility of discriminatory treatment, and (ii) The Constitution confers various positive rights or what is known as affirmative actions to members of minority groups.

It is the latter, i.e., positive discrimination or special provisions that has created more debate than the former one which aims at bringing about a concrete change in the lives of the minority communities. To ensure non-discrimination as guaranteed in the Constitution, it is necessary that special procedures, institutions and arrangements have to be established through which members of minorities are able to make decisions, exercise legislature and administrative powers and in order to develop their culture.

Special provisions or positive discrimination should be understood in the context of Special Rights. Human Rights: Minority Rights mention in regard into special rights mention, "Special rights are not privileges but they are granted to make it possible for minorities to preserve their identity, characteristics and traditions. Special rights are just as important in achieving equality of treatment as non-discrimination . . . this form of affirmative action may have to be sustained over a prolonged period in order to enable minority groups to benefit from society on an equal footing with the majority." Such minority representation rights are taken as democratic means of democratization in a social and political structure which create inequalities and injustice. Minority rights protected them from the possibility of discriminatory treatment and also confers some positive rights (or what is known as affirmative actions) on members of minority groups which they shared with other citizens of the country.

The special provisions in the Constitution are as follows:

- *Article 14* of the Indian Constitution confers equality before laws and declares that all persons are equal before law.
- *Article 15* says that no citizen shall be discriminated on grounds of religion, race, caste, sex or place of birth etc.
- *Article 16* mentions equality of opportunity in matters of public employment.
- *Article 25* provides the fundamental rights to freedom of conscience and the right freely to profess, practice and propagate religion.
- *Article 26* talks of freedom to manage religious affairs given to religious denominations or sections thereof.
- *Article 27* ensures that no one should be compelled to pay any taxes, the proceeds of which are specifically appropriated in payment of expenses for the promotion or maintenance of any particular religion or religious denominations.
- *Article 28* speaks about freedom to attendance at religious instructions or religious workshop in certain educational institutions.

- *Article 29 and 30* guarantee cultural and educational rights of the minorities. Section I, Article 29 mentions, "Any section of the citizens residing in the territory of India or any part thereof having a distinct language, script or culture of its own shall have the right to conserve the same."
- *Article 30* (Right to Constitutional Remedies) mentions about remedies for enforcement of rights conferred to move the Supreme Court for seeking justice. Article 30, Section (i) mentions all minorities, whether based on religion or language shall have the right to establish and administer educational institutions of their choice. Section (2) provides the state shall not, in granting aid to educational institutions, discriminate against any educational institution on the ground that is under the management of a minority whether based on religion or language.

Our Constitution provides for the protection of the interests of linguistic minorities. Article 350-A imposes a duty on the state of endeavour to provide adequate facilities for instruction in the mother tongue at the primary stage of education to children belonging to linguistic minority. Article 350-B gives the power to President to appoint a special officer for linguistic minorities to investigate matters relating to the safeguards provided for linguistic minorities under the condition.

CONCLUSION

Minority rights and backwardness among the minorities have become central issues of discourse in India. Ambrose Pinto S.J. says, "Right from the independence struggle, the relationship of the minority with majority community, that is Muslims, has been conflict-ridden. The changes in the political and social life in the last five decades of independence with political parties competing for votes and the emergence of Hindutva politics in the last one decade has made the tension and conflicts more visible. Included in the list, especially from the seventies for target and attack were Sikhs and in the nineties, the Christian community. Damage has been done to Buddhists and Jains as well by including them in the Hindu religion and robbing them of their specific identity. In the midst of such attacks on religious minorities, the endeavour here is to examine reason behind such attitudes of the Indian state on minorities and the approach minorities might adopt towards the state in the situation."

A definite mindset formed out of continuous interaction between minority and majority arises majority-minority dichotomy. The minorities are subjected to discrimination deprivation and marginalization in the society and polity where the majority enjoy dominance and supremacy. Other basic issues are that the majority enjoy dominance and supremacy. Other basic issues affecting the lives of minorities are poverty, resourcelessness and constraints on self-determination.

Although the Constitution of India has recognized the necessity of providing both positive discrimination ensuring affirmative action for the upliftment and welfare of the minorities and also impose negative injunctions against every form of discrimination, differentiation and marginalization of the minorities.

These constitutional provisions have been misused by the political leaders to further their own end. Moreover, positive discrimination or special provisions have created more debate than any concrete change in the lives of the minority communities. It is to be considered that these minority rights are a means to abridge the gap between the advantaged and the disadvantaged segments of the society and once the necessary equilibrium in political, economic social sphere is reached, preferential treatment does not remain important. Rights are a means to development of all the sections of the society and not an exclusive domain of any particular segment of society.

THE MINORITY COMMISSION

In order to ensure effective enforcement and implementation of the rights of minorities, the Government of India set up Minorities Commission in January, 1978. Later, the Parliament enacted the National Commission for Minorities Act, 1992 which assigned a statutory status to the Commission and renamed it as National Commission for Minorities (NCM).

The Resolution of the Commission mentions:

> Despite the safeguards provided in the Constitution and the laws in force, there persists amongst the minorities a feeling of inequality and discrimination. In order to preserve secular traditions and to promote national integration the government of India attaches the highest importance to the enforcement of the safeguards provided for the minorities and is of the firm view that effective institutional arrangements are urgently required for the effective enforcement and implementation of all the safeguards provided for the minorities in the Constitution, in central and states laws, and in Government policies and administrative schemes enunciated from time to time.

The Commission explains minorities as "Group held together by ties of common descent, language or religious faith, and feelings themselves different in their respects from the majority of the inhabitants of a given entity." The Commission carries out the following special functions:

(i) to evaluate the working of the various safeguards provided in the Constitution for the protection of minorities and in laws passed by the Union and State government;

(ii) to make recommendations with a view to ensuring effective implementation and reinforcement of all the safeguards and the laws;

(iii) to undertake a review of the implementation of the politics pursued by the union and the state governments with respect to the minorities;

(iv) to look into specific complaints regarding deprivation of rights and safeguards of the minorities;

(v) to conduct studies, research and analyse on the question of avoidance of discrimination against minorities;

(vi) to suggest appropriate legal and welfare measures in respect of any minority to be undertaken by the centre or the state government;

(vii) to serve as a national clearing house for information in respect of the conditions of the minorities.

(viii) To make provided reports at prescribed intervals to the government.

The achievements of the Minority Commission are as follows:

Statutory Status to the State Minority Commissions

In the first meeting of the new Commission held on 9th March, 2000, the Commission addressed those State Government/Union Territories had not established State Minorities Commission or those who had not vested in them a statutory status. The Commission wrote to the respective State governments like Karnataka, Delhi, Gujarat etc. and government of Union Territories accordingly.

The Government of Karnataka has set up a Separate Minorities Welfare Department, in response to the Commission's standing recommendation to this effect. On the recommendation of the Commission, such Departments have been set up in Andhra Pradesh (1993), Uttar Pradesh (1996), West Bengal (1996) and Assam (1998).

The Government of Delhi has set up a three-member ad-hoc State Minorities Commission. On 14th July, 1999, a meeting with the members of the newly set up Delhi State Minorities Commission was held in the NCM. A Draft-Bill for giving it statutory status prepared on the model of the NCM Act, 1992 was examined in depth on the State Government's request and finalised.

The Gujarat Minorities Board functioning since 1981 was elevated to a Corporation by the previous State Government, but the implementation of the decision was withheld by the present Government. On the recommendation of the NCM, the State Government has now finally given it the status of a Corporation.

Statutory Recommendations of the Commission

The Commission has made the following statutory recommendations under the NCM Act which has a bearing on policy formulation in the Government:

(i) The Commission on 27.11.2001 to the State Government of Uttar Pradesh reiterated that compensation to the next of the kin of those killed in the riots should be enhanced to Rs. 2 lakhs as recommended earlier vide circular letter dated 25 November, 1997 to all the State Governments and Union Territories;

(ii) The Commission recommended to the Reserve Bank of India on 12.09.2001 that there should be free flow of loan to minorities including Muslims from the Nationalised Banks;

(iii) The National Commission for Minorities recommended 20.06.2001 that the Government of India, Minority of Finance should evolve and implement a Central Interest Subsidy Scheme for communal riot affected borrowers of the minority communities including Muslims in all future communal riots, on the pattern of the existing Central Interest Subsidy Scheme for 1984 riot affected Sikh borrowers;

(iv) The Commission recommended to the Archaeological Survey of India on 06.06.2001 that entry to religious places and shrines be exempted from entry fees.

(v) The Commission recommended on 21.06.2001 to all

the State Governments that adequate legal provisions be made to facilitate nomination for each of the five minority communities in the Upper Houses of the State Legislatures;

(vi) The Commission on 31.11.2000 recommended to the Railway Board that the railway fare concessions available to students of recognized educational institutions be also extended to Madarsas, which normally do not seek Governmental recognition.

Minority Communities

The erstwhile Ministry of Welfare now Ministry of Social Justice and Empowerment issued Notification dated 23rd October, 1993. The Notification is reproduced below:

> "In exercise of powers conferred by Clause (c) of Section 2 of the National Commission for Minorities Act, 1992 (19 of 1992), the Central Government hereby notifies the following communities as "the minority communities" for the purposes of the said Act, namely:
>
> 1. Muslims
> 2. Christians
> 3. Sikhs
> 4. Buddhists
> 5. Zoroastrians (Parsis)

Percentage of Minority viz-a-viz Majority

Minorities in India as per National Commission for Minorities Act, 1992 are Muslims, Christians, Buddhists, Sikhs and Parsis. As per 1991 census, these communities constitute about 17.5 per cent of the total population of the country numbering about 14.8 crores. The population statistics as per 1991 census for the entire country comes to 84.45 crores. The majority population constitute 82.5 per cent (69.65 crores), whereas the minority population constitute 17.5 per cent (14.80 crores).

The Community wise population is estimated as Muslims—71 per cent, Christians—13 per cent, Sikhs—11 per cent, Buddhists—4 per cent and Parsis—1 per cent.

Dr. Gopal Singh in a study report on Minorities submitted to Government in 1983 has clearly brought out that amongst poorest of the poor Minorities constitute the majority.

The National Commission for Minorities has constituted a Minority Education cell to exclusively look into the problems being faced by Minority Educational Institutions in regard to recognition, affiliation, grants-in-aids etc.

CHAPTER 4

The Central Backward Classes Commission

India in pursuance with its ideal to create a modern welfare egalitarian state is committed to the upliftment and welfare of the backward sections of the society. It was necessary to bring the downtrodden and neglected into the main-stream and a device used for it was the realisation of the principle of preferential treatment or positive discrimination. The Constitution of India provides for the recognition of socially backward classes. For this, Article 340 is there for appointment of a Commission to investigate the conditions of backward classes.

(a) The President may by order appoint a Commission consisting of such persons as he thinks fit to investigate the conditions of socially and educationally backward classes within the territory of India and the difficulties under which they labour and to make recommendations as to the steps that should be taken by the Union or any State to remove such difficulties and to improve their condition and as to the grants that should be made for the purpose by the Union or any State and the conditions subject to which such grants should be made, and the order appointing such Commission shall define the procedure to be followed by the Commission.

(b) A Commission so appointed shall investigate the matters referred to them and present to the President a report setting out the facts as found by them and making such recommendations as they think proper.

(c) The President shall cause a copy of the report so presented together with a memorandum explaining the action taken thereon to be laid before each House of Parliament.

(d) Permanent Commissions should be appointed within four months by the Central Government and the State Governments to decide regularly the cases which would arise involving questions whether a particular caste or section of a caste was rightly included or excluded; and all further proceedings in such 'matters can be taken only in the Supreme Court.'

(e) "Backward caste cannot be determined only and exclusively with reference to economic criterion, ... and therefore, the 10 per cent additional reservations made by the second memorandum of 25 September, 1991 was illegal and void.

(f) Armed forces and some higher civilian posts to be selected by the government should be outside the purview of caste reservations.

(g) Reservations cannot be applied to promotions, "crutches cannot be provided throughout one's career."

Article 340 provides for the appointment of Commission to investigate the conditions of socially and educationally backward classes and the difficulties under which they labour.

Panchayati Raj Institutions are local government bodies scheduled established under the Constitution. Under Article 243D, one-third of seats reserved for Scheduled Castes and Tribes, are reserved for women, and one-third (including the number of seats reserved for women belonging to the Scheduled Castes and the Scheduled Tribes) of the total number of seats to be filled by direct election in every Panchayat are reserved for women.

The State is required to foster respect for international law and treaty obligations and Parliament has the power to make laws implementing international agreements (articles 51(c) and 253). There are proposals to reserve seats for women in the House of the People and in the Legislative Assemblies of the Sates by amending the Constitution.

The Constitution of India gave a special mandate to the President of India under Article 341(1) to specify the castes, or races under a Schedule. The castes as listed become eligible for the purposes of discriminatory protections and favours designed for that purpose.

In the past, two Commissions were appointed, in exercise of the powers conferred under Article 340 of the Constitution, by the President of India, to determine the criteria to be adopted for considering sections of the people as socially and educationally backward classes. The first Commission headed by Kakasaheb Kalelkar was setup in 1950 and the second Commission, headed by B.P. Mandal, was appointed in 1978.

These Commissions submitted Reports in March 1955 and December 1980. While determining the criteria for defining socially and educationally backward classes both the Commissions accepted caste as the main basis for determining backwardness.

CENTRAL BACKWARD CLASSES COMMISSION

The first Backward Classes Commission was established under the Chairmanship of Kaka Saheb Kalelkar consisting of 11 members on January 29, 1953 by the President of India. The Commission was entrusted with the task to determine the criteria for the identification of the backward communities, investing their conditions and recommending measures for their upliftment. The Commission adopted different criteria like the social, educational, representational and economic namely:

(i) Low social position in the traditional caste hierarchy of Hindu Society.

(ii) Lack of general educational advancement among the major section of a caste or community.

(iii) Inadequate or no representation in government services.

(iv) Inadequate representation in the field of trade, commerce and industry.

Kalelkar Commission submitted the report incorporating a list of 2399 backward castes or communities for the entire country. Since there was a difference of opinion among the Commission members on number of issues of the acceptance of caste as basis for preparing the list of the backward classes and its emphasis on economic tests. The Report was not accepted by the Central Government and so not implemented except being used for reference and academic purposes.

On 7 August, 1990, Prime Minister V.P. Singh announced in the House the decision taken by the Government to implement the Mandal Commission Report. As a result, an Office Memorandum was issued by the Department of Personnel and Training, Ministry of Personnel, Public Grievances and Pensions on 13 August, 1991 addressed to all Ministers, Departments of the Government of India and Public Sectors Undertakings extending benefits to the socially and educationally backward classes (SEBC) as opined by the Commission in the services of Union and the Public Undertakings. According to it, 27 per cent of the vacancies in civil posts and services under the Government of India were declared reserved for SEBC, to be filled by direct recruitment.

The Mandal Commission report was to be implemented in toto and without any dilution. But the implementation of its recommendations was challenged and opposed not only by angry students belonging to Hindu Upper Castes, but also by the Supreme Court Bar Association. The Federation of Indian

Chambers of Commerce and Industry (FICCI) and the Associated Chambers of Commerce and Industry (ASSOCHAM) opposed the job quota. Its joint statement mentioned that the founders of the Constitution never expected that the reservations would last forever or it would be extended to other classes.

Acceptance of caste as a criterion for social backwardness was vehemently opposed by some members of the Kalelkar Commission in their notes of dissent. In the forwarding letter to the President, Kakasaheb Kalelkar, the Chairman of the Commission had mentioned that "his eyes were opened to the dangers of suggesting remedies on the caste basis when he discovered that it is going to have a most unhealthy effect on the Muslim and Christian section of the nation." The recommendations of the majority members of the Commission was a 'rude shock' to the Chairman Kakesaheb Kalelkar. "It drove him to the conclusion that the remedies suggested in the Report of the Commission were worst than the evil which they were out to combat." The report of Kalelkar Commission was rejected by the then Central Government as it felt that "it would be better to apply economic tests than to go by Castes." It was thereafter left to the discretion of the State Government to choose their own criteria for defining backwardness. Several States did set up their own Commissions or Committees for defining the criteria for backwardness and on the basis of such reports provided reservations under Article 15(4) and 16(4) of the Constitution. Some of these States agreed to treat Muslim community as backward class as a result of which the Muslims in these States could avail the benefit of reservations.

When the Janata Party Government came in power at the Centre, with Morarji Desai as Prime Minister and Atal Behari Vajpayee and L.K. Advani as Ministers of External Affairs and Information respectively, the issue was reopened by the Centre.

The Second Backward Classes Commission was appointed under the provision of Article 340 of the Constitution after a long gap by Prime Minister Morarji Desai on 20 December, 1978, under the Chairmanship of Bindhyeshwari Prasad

Mandal, former Chief Minister of Bihar consisting of four members. The Mandal Commission evolved eleven criteria under the three headings, social, economic and education, to identify the degree of backwardness. A special weightage was given to all these criteria i.e. three points each were given to form social indicators, two points to each of the three educational indicators and one point to each of the four economic indicators. A score of 11 points or more of the total 22 points was considered necessary for listing castes/classes as socially and educationally backward. The Commission submitted its report on 31 December, 1980 and enlisted 3,743 castes/communities as OBCs.

The Mandal Commission report applied to:

(i) All employment, civil or military, under the government,

(ii) To employment in all Public Sector enterprises,

(iii) To Private Sector enterprises which in any manner receive any financial assistance from the state or any Public Sector Undertaking,

(iv) To admission and engagement in all Universities and affiliated Colleges, and

(v) To promotion to all levels in the areas covered and by (i) to (iv) above.

The Mandal Commission arrived at the figure of 52 per-cent of India's population as belonging to the category of OBCs and recommended reservation in educational institutions and employment to the extent of 27 per cent so as to top the limit as indicated by the Supreme Court.

The Mandal Commission came to the conclusion that 66.26 per cent of the total population of India consisted of Backward Hindu Castes (including 22.56 per cent SC and ST) and that Forward Hindu Castes and communities accounted for only 17.58 per cent. Total Hindu population was estimated to be 83.84 per cent. The population of Non-Hindus (Muslims,

Christians, Sikhs, Buddhists and Jains) was estimated to be 16.16 per cent.

The above findings of Mandal Commission means that 79 per cent of the Hindus belong to Backward Castes and that only 21 per cent of the Hindus (Brahmins, Bhumihars, Rajputs, Marathas, Jats, Vaishyas-Banias, Kayastha etc.) are Forward Class Hindus. The Commission, however, proceeded on the 'assumption' that only 52 per cent of the Non-Hindu religious Groups were backward.

While making its final recommendations the Mandal Commission had accepted Caste as a criterion for identifying backwardness among the Hindus as it felt that" Castes are the building bricks of Hindu social structure."

For identifying backwardness among the Non-Hindus the Commission had identified the following criteria:

(i) All untouchables converted to any Non-Hindu - Religion; and

(ii) Such occupational communities which are known by the name of their traditional hereditary occupation and whose Hindu counterparts have been included in the list of Hindu OBCs (such as Dhobi, Teli, Dheemar, Nai, Gujjar, Kumhar, Lohar, Darji, Badhai etc.).

Mandal Commission was conspicuously silent on the issue of declaring the Muslim Community as a whole a Backward community. Very few Muslims were however deemed by the Mandal Commission eligible to be included in the list of Other Backward Classes in the Non-Hindu Categories.

In addition to the prevailing reservations of 22.5 per cent for the SCs and STs (in proportion to their population) the Mandal Commission had recommended reservation of 27 per-cent for Other Backward Classes thereby increasing the quantum of reservations from 22.5 per cent to 49.5 per cent. The Commission had further recommended that "States which have already introduced reservations for OBCs exceeding 27 per cent will remain unaffected by this recommendation."

In several cases the Supreme Court of India has held that the quantum of reservations under Articles 15(4) and 16(4) should remain below 50 per cent. Under the above circumstances there appears to be hardly any scope for any further reservation for the Muslims or any other religious community unless the Constitution of India is suitably amended or the recommendations of the Mandal Commission are suitably revised by the Government at the Centre.

In some States as a result of the recommendations of Mandal Commission the quantum of reservation exceeds the limits of 50 per cent. This is considered to be unconstitutional. In its 1999 Election Manifesto the National Democratic Alliance has promised that the "reservation percentages, above 50 per cent, as followed by certain states shall be sanctified through necessary legislative measures." Nothing has, however, been done so far by the National Democratic Alliance Government at the Centre and the stalemate still continues.

In these judgments, the Supreme Court partially upholds the memoranda but subject to qualifications and conditions and secondly, declares that these memoranda providing for reservations on caste basis are unconstitutional and void.

CONCLUSION

The Mandal Commission Reports and the action taken after 1990 have made the politics of backwardness a major national phenomenon. The reservation politics have produced considerable redistributive efforts although these are not spared evenly to the intended beneficiary groups. Social, economic and educational reforms will go a long way to provide justice to the 'backward' communities who have remained oppressed.

Now, the total reservation quota stands at 45 per cent in many States of India and this includes the SCs, STs and the OBCs. There is a shift of trend towards reverse discrimination rather than mere affirmative action. A few backward class elites have gained political or economic power based on reservations.

But the majority of the backward classes are living on margin and their subsistence is meagre. The undeserving people gain advantages and the deserving ones are still without a significant change in their situation. Still, the creamy layer of every caste which have usurped most of the privileges of reservations have seen to it that the privileges do not reach to the most backwards. The caste which refused to be declared as backward at in the first one' or two decades of Independence are not vying with each other to be so declared as they want to take advantage of being 'backward' for the "caste badge" has become a relevant factor. Moreover everyday, the list of backward caste including that of Scheduled Castes and Scheduled Tribes is increasing, so much so, there has already been 90 per cent increase in the number of centrally notified OBCs that have been raised from 1,257 castes in 1993 to 2,297 in 2006. Also the issue of 'faking caste' has been on an increase due to reasons like corruption and poor administrative set up. The sectoral parties have a vested interest in keeping backward communities backward in order to ensure their support and thus, working against their progress. The vote bank equations compel the political parties to retain and enhance the demand of reservation related beneficiaries. Myron Weiner remarks, "so many groups within the electorate now benefit from reservations that policy reversal is politically unlikely."

The recent HRD ministry proposal to increase the reservations for Backward groups in universities to 49.5 per cent on 5 April, 2006 to incorporate OBCs in all central government institutes of higher education in 2006 has caused a great deal of controversy and led to protests by various segments of people areas the country especially the student community. In globalised world there is a need to reduce the existing reservations in the educational institutions for it would seriously undermine merit and quality.

CHAPTER 5

Problem of Positive Discrimination

In the last five-six decade so much has been written on reservation, it evokes a sense of intellectual exhaustion, if not despair. Most people are of the view that the arguments are by now fairly well-drawn between the pro-reservation and the anti-reservation lobbies and arguments on both sides are well-known and well-rehearsed. That may be so; yet, despite the many face-offs between the two sides, there has been an intense dialogue on this subject. Dialogue requires, among other things, an environment in which questions can be freely raised, and objections listened to and addressed with sincerity rather than polemic and ridicule—a condition that has not always been met in the debates on reservations.

Dialogue has also been made difficult by the fact that reservations received a constitutional sanction. In sharp contrast to most other liberal democracies, the Constitution of India provided for equality before the law as well as equality of opportunity. Article 16 of the Constitution, referring to equality of opportunity in matters of public employment, made a provision for reservation of posts for 'backward class of citizens'. This did not simply accord legal sanction to the reservations; it suggested that the principle of equality of opportunity is readily compatible with the policy of reservations. Since no qualifying conditions were stipulated the this fostered the impression that reservation of seats, at least in the public sector was, what might following Rawls be called, a 'constitutional essential'. As such it required little deliberation on the issue nor needed justification of any kind.

The situation became more complicated as governments in power, both at the Centre as well as the states, used the available constitutional clause to bracket all issues of social and distributive justice into that of reservations. Politically assertive and opportunist groups also translated their demands into claims for reservations. In a situation of acute scarcity of desirable goods, reservations became an important asset for accessing valuable resources. The ensuing competition for, and escalation in, the demand for reservations created a division that subsequently became the focus of concern and debate.

Not only did this limit the possibility of any dialogue between the adversarial positions, it also shifted attention from the primary question, 'How should we pursue the task of social justice in a hierarchical and highly stratified society?' to the effects of the policy of reservations. While some analysts saw reservations as reinforcing caste identities and compromising merit or efficiency, others dismissed these arguments. They interpreted these statements as expressing the anxiety of the upper castes who feared the social transformation unleashed by reservations. Either way, fundamental questions pertaining to the agenda of distributive justice, the purpose of affirmative action policies and the place of reservations or quotas within that framework, remained largely unattended.

Statements by members of the present government relating to the extension of reservations to the private sector have once again brought the issue of reservations to the centre-stage. They have, in addition to the persisting concerns about distributive justice, affirmative action and quotas, raised serious legal and theoretical problems. The Constitution made provisions for reservation of seats in public employment. It left the private domain out which is now being targeted.

In a liberal democracy no area of life can claim to be outside the purview of law and, by extension, of governmental regulation. From family to industry, all fall under the watchful eye of the law. The world over the law regulates, in varying degree, the relationships of the members of the household; it lays down the limits of what is and is not permissible in the house as much as it does for the open outdoors. Hence, in principle nothing is exempt from public scrutiny and deliberation, but all such interventions in a liberal democracy are justified only when they are aimed at enhancing either the liberty of citizens or fairness of a contract.

In each case the object of state action are procedural aspects, the idea being that substantive ends within the wider principle of equal liberty for all will be left to individuals and particular entities. Policies involving reservation of seats almost always raise liberal anxieties as they blur this distinction and involve prescription of a desired end. While this does not mean that such policies have no place in a liberal framework, it does suggest that reservation of seats require careful consideration; more specifically, they need to be formulated and pursued in a way that fits well with other values cherished in a liberal democracy and enshrined in the Constitution.

All public policies entail a fine balance between the different values affirmed in the Constitution of a country. The need for this may be more compelling in the case of reservation policy but is by no means peculiar to it. The Constitution of India made space for framing policies involving reservations while affirming the commitment to equality of opportunity. The most basic requirement then is to ensure that reservations do not erode or negate the principle of equal opportunity. To put it in another way, the first question is, how can reservations function in a way that enhances, or at least, respects the principle of equality of opportunity?

The courts have addressed this constitutional necessity by stipulating an upper limit for the seats reserved in institutions and jobs. This is an important step but it still requires consideration of the grounds that enable us to reconcile the principle of equal opportunity with the policy of reservations. In theory this reconciliation is effected by the arguments that (a) reservations seek to ensure a level playing field, and (b) they only seek to compensate those who have suffered harm due to past practices of the society as a whole. Open competition and equal opportunity entail that the race or the competition be fair. If the odds favour some in advance then both the principle of fairness as well as equality of opportunity is violated. Affirmative action, including positive discrimination, enter into the picture here as measures seeking to ensure that no one has a head start in the race.

Gurpreet Mahajan expresses, "Affirmative action can take many different forms and may include a wide range of actions—from formulation of anti-discrimination laws and access to social and public goods to special consideration in various spheres of social and institutional life. Further, special consideration may take different forms. It may involve preferential spending, positive weightings, or reservation of seats in favour of the disadvantaged sections. Reservations is, thus, one of the many kinds of affirmative actions that the state may pursue and it is one that is best seen as a way of supplementing other forms of affirmative action rather than a stand-alone policy. In India, the positive discrimination, right from the beginning has taken mainly the form of reserved seats, to which the "eligible candidates can gain access without competing with candidates from non-eligible groups" and these "beneficiary groups are often entitled to their proportion of reserved seats or positions over and above the number that they gain in open competition."

Thus, if seats are reserved for the disadvantaged sections in educational institutions, then the success of this measure rests crucially upon the existence of other enabling conditions that help children to develop skills and capacities which are essential for performing well in the school. In England and America, for instance, governments often spend money in developing the infrastructural facilities in weak and poor neighbourhoods. They build playgrounds, libraries and community centres so that children here have access to resources that the children of the relatively rich enjoy and which channel their energies constructively, while simultaneously giving them an opportunity to hone skills that enable better performance in schools. Such forms of preferential spending are sometimes as important as measures of reservation of seats. In fact, most often they make the difference between a successful and an unsuccessful affirmative action programme.

Affirmative action programmes thus entail a range of policies other than reservations. What needs also to be emphasized is that reservation by itself may be a rather limited form of affirmative action which would of necessity rely more on increasing quotas and lowering the benchmark at all levels rather than providing access to disadvantaged sections on an equal footing. Given the recent tendency to equate affirmative action with reservations, it is equally necessary to recognize that there can be affirmative action agendas even without reservations. As we deliberate on reservation policy today, we need both to accept the need for affirmative action policies as well as to acknowledge some of the weaknesses of the existing policies on reservations.

Two other aspects of the thinking on reservations require serious consideration. First, in India particularly, reservations have often been associated with the absence of merit and efficiency in the workplace. This view has won some legitimacy because of the way the policy is currently practiced. When qualifications are often lowered for those who come in through the reserved quota, the impression created is that merit is being set aside. In a situation where seats are reserved without fulfilling other associated conditions, such as, quality education, reduction in the benchmark is bound to occur.

But this need not be the case, and shortcomings in the existing policy should not be the basis for assessing the policy of reservations. Reservation of seats *per se* does not require lowering of standards. All it suggests is that all things being more or less equal, a person in the identified category must receive preference. In any case it does not imply that someone without merit and necessary competence would be given the job. Similarly, there is no reason to assume that the communities now being included are without merit and talent. If anything, history provides considerable proof that these groups bring with them new resources and perspectives that enrich public and social life.

Hence, anxieties about reservations bringing in mediocrity or inefficiency are quite misplaced and they confuse the accidental with the necessary condition. At the same time it needs reiteration that arguments coming from the other side are equally unsatisfactory. The claim that reservations in jobs and positions are justified because these communities have been excluded for centuries is indeed problematic. It invokes the principle of compensatory justice and suggests that communities previously harmed must now be suitably compensated.

There is no doubt that communities that have been the victims of forced segregation have been harmed, yet the language of compensation does not provide an adequate justification for positive discrimination in favour of these victims. Principles of compensatory justice rely on pinpointing clearly the victim and the victimizer and the precise nature of the harm done by the latter to the former. This creates several difficulties as the degree of harm suffered may vary within the identified community.

Even when all the victims are supposed to be harmed equally, it remains to be seen whether all the other members of society were victimizers. If some fought alongside the victims for their freedom should they be treated as victimizers and expected to sacrifice seats and positions? Reservations, which are the strongest expression of positive discrimination, cannot therefore be justified adequately on grounds of compensation for past injustices.

There is need to address the issue of existing inequalities and continuing injustice. But neither arguments relying on compensation nor those using the language of rectifying past wrongs offer viable answers. Indeed, as Hegel reminds us, in the act of rectifying past wrongs we may create new wrongs. Consequently, as we work to create a society that is free from existing structures of inequality and hierarchy, these moral vocabularies that posit reservations as matters of right, or as being intrinsically 'right' or 'wrong', need to be replaced with a framework where we have a reasoned evaluation of what is appropriate, or unwise, in the pursuit of a given goal in a specific context.

Greek philosopher, Aristotle maintained that engagement in politics required men with practical wisdom, who would deliberate both on the ends to be pursued as well as the appropriate means of realizing those goals. The idea being that what may be necessary and reasonable in one context may not be so in another. Each situation, therefore, calls for a reasoned evaluation rather than the application of a pre-given truth.

This is the perspective from which we need to approach the issue of reservations and debate the extension of reservations to new categories of recipients and to new areas of economy and polity. It is pertinent here to recall that policies of affirmative action have a long history in India but when the Constitution of independent India made space for them it was not on account of retaining some continuity with the past. If anything, it was the desire to create a society very different from that which existed in the past that prompted such measures as reservations of seats.

Reservations provided to the Scheduled Castes and the Scheduled Tribes were visualized as an instrument of inclusion. Ambedkar, who played a crucial role here, feared that existing social prejudices would result in the continued exclusion of the Scheduled Castes from the political process. This is why he advocated reservations as a special measure to bring in the voice of the erstwhile excluded and segregated populations in the decision-making process.

The inclusion of these communities in the public services was similarly expected to fulfil an essential condition of democracy. Ambedkar felt that the absence of the 'depressed' communities from public services, such as, police and local administration, might imply that the atrocities against them would remain unregistered and unacknowledged. Hence, it was to ensure that these communities can exercise their rights as equals that reservations were favoured in the public services. The fact that these measures of inclusion were likely to bestow a range of additional benefits, such as, social and occupational mobility, new role models for members of the community, a sense of dignity and respect, were significant but these were in the nature of derivative goods. The primary reason for reservations was the goal of inclusion in the face of existing social prejudice.

It was evident to him that reservations could not erase existing prejudice; indeed their purpose was not to end social prejudice. He knew that social prejudices that had operated in society for thousands of years would not vanish in ten years. Yet, he insisted that reservations should be time bound and that at the end of ten years the policy should be assessed by the Parliament. Ambedkar recognized that policies of reservation that seek to enhance equality are envisaged as temporary measures whose continuation or extension needed to be discussed and debated with the change in context and circumstances.

The Scheduled Tribes were in many ways different from the Scheduled Castes, but in their case too reservations were a way of including them into the polity. Without reservations in legislative bodies, many felt that their distinctive needs and perspective might remain unrepresented. In both cases reservations were linked to overcoming legal and social barriers in the path of political participation and representation. Reservations were, in this sense, an instrument for the effective functioning of democracy.

Over the last 58 years the policies on reservations have changed significantly and this has yielded several paradoxes that needs careful consideration. Perhaps the most striking and far-reaching change has come in the rationale for seeking and granting reservations. If inclusion was the primary concern earlier, it is adequate representation and social transformation that justify reservations and generate new demands for the extension of this policy. Two things have occurred as a consequence of this. The first is that the democratic commitment to inclusion of targeted communities that had suffered on account of forced exclusion or segregation. The concern for social transformation has thrown the doors open to many new categories of deprived groups and communities. Since the latter focuses less on the cause of deprivation and more on the circumstances of deprivation, demands for reservations have steadily increased.

Secondly, the changed rationale has placed a question mark against caste-based reservations. Since caste was the ground on which some communities had previously been excluded and segregated, caste offered an appropriate criterion for identifying those who needed to be included as equals. However, when the concern shifts to minimizing backwardness or deprivation, the relevance of caste as the basis of identifying beneficiaries itself becomes debatable. While there may be a correlation between low caste and low income, there are groups in every religion and caste that are deprived. Should they not receive some consideration? In other words, the changing concerns of the reservation policy raises the question about' what constitutes 'backwardness'? Is income and wealth a more adequate basis for identifying the least advantaged in society? If, however, caste remains the operative criterion, should we not distinguish between members who are better off than the rest of the community.

These questions arise sharply in the context of the shift in the thinking on reservations. But they reveal the contradictions and limitations in the existing policy framework. The focus on transformation and development also raises the issue of the efficacy of reservations as a policy. Pitted against the structural change affected by policies like land reforms on the one hand, and the potential created by the growing political presence of the marginalized populations even in the absence of reservations, the need to rely on reservations for achieving the goal of social transformation has itself become a matter of dispute. Today, both the continuance of the policy of reservations and the manner of its operation require public debate. It is not as if the consensus around reservations has broken down, but that fresh consensus has to be built through reasoned arguments between contending viewpoints.

As we consider the necessity of extending reservations for identified communities in the private sector, we need to reflect carefully on the rationale of reservations as well as consider the best possible way of achieving the desired goal of social justice within the framework outlined, by the Constitution. This task acquires greater urgency when we consider that the Constitution affirmed equality before the law and equality of opportunity; it provided space for formulating policies of reservations but spoke only of public services in this regard. Concerns of representation and inclusion are compelling when we are dealing with public institutions of a democratic polity but the same cannot be said about the private sector. Hence, as we formulate policies for the latter in an increasingly liberalizing economy, accommodating the values enshrined in the Constitution with the concerns of social justice may require a willingness to innovate and explore new ideas and policy perspectives.

At the theoretical level, we have rarely considered the possibility of using anti-discrimination laws to pursue the ideal of equal opportunity. Likewise, we have not given sufficient attention to the role of affirmative action, other than reservations. Reservations in turn have remained delinked from other policies involving redistribution of material goods; and the role that distribution of non-material goods can play in promoting social justice has remained neglected. So far affirmative action programmes have been prompted by the concern for equality. Should they now be applied to promote diversity? What policies would be required for pursuing the ideal of diversity as distinct from that of equality? Either way, what must remain inviolable if the principle of equality before the law is to have any meaning at all?

If these are a few of the conceptual and theoretical issues that face us, problems presented by the existing policy packages involving affirmative action and reservations are many more. To analyze the latter we would need to take cognizance of the diverse range of policies initiated in different states along with the changes that have gradually been introduced through the acts of various commissions and the judicial institutions. The enormity of the task ahead only underlines the urgency to take a step, however small, in this direction. Dialogue is not just a political necessity of the hour; it is an essential and indispensable condition of policy formulation: one that makes a crucial difference between politics and public affairs in a democracy.

CHAPTER 6

The Politics of Reservation in Education

THE PHILOSOPHICAL FOUNDATIONS OF A JUST SOCIETY

Our Constitution elucidates the foundations of a social order - based on "Justice, Liberty. Equality and Fraternity." The Directive Principles of State Policy aspires to create a level playing are given special treatment. Veerappa Moily, while defining the parameters of a just society says, "While Equality, Justice and Fraternity provide the foundations of a just social order, Liberty provides the underlying principle to bring out the best in individual members of the society while Justice relates to the society and Liberty relates to the individual, the power paves the way to establishing an inclusive society and the latter finds the path for the individual in pursuit of excellence." There should be a balance between these two cardinal principles of Justice and Liberty while more and more people are provided access to higher education.

Education aims to ensure serial inclusion and academic excellence. When all the components of the state remain in harmony, the society is just. An unjust society is which keeps a large section of its people in a state of denial or deprivation or where all its citizens do not enjoy equality of opportunity to develop themselves. And the best way to empower the excluded sections of the society is to provide access to higher education. Plato said that what Education enables is to "prepare a citizen, by the light of knowledge and not by rule of custom, to perform the duties of his station."

RESERVATIONS FOR SCs, STs AND OBCs

The idea of egalitarian society was envisaged by the founding fathers of our Constitution, the basic document of governance in India. The Constitution of India, which came into force in 1950, mandated 15 per cent reservation for the Scheduled Castes (SCs) and 7.5 per cent for the Scheduled Tribes (STs).

The rationale behind positive discrimination in favour of the Scheduled Castes (SCs) and the Scheduled Tribes (STs) or the India's Dalits or Adivasis is that they had been denied equality for long and reservations are a form of compensation for their long history of mistreatment and discrimination on the part of the majority population.

Moreover, if India has to emerge as an economic giant in the 21st century, the SCs, the STs and the OBCs have to be equally equipped as any other section of the society. For this it is imperative its educated our young population. They should not only be made literate, but also trained to take up technical jobs. An eminent demographer Ashish Bose said, "India needs schools, the best schools at primary, secondary and higher secondary levels.' We have to specially strive to equip the SC, ST and OBC children to develop their capabilities to get a fair deal and also to integerate and empower them. The government also has to give especial incentives at the higher education level. Saroj K. Poddar comments, "A financial support system must in place so that students from under-represented communities, who gain admissions to higher educational institutions, are not constrained by lack of funds."

The Constitution of India is designed to provide and protect reservations in the educational institutions.

In centrally controlled higher education institutions in India 15 per cent of the seats are reserved for the SC members and 7.5 per cent for ST members and in the case of higher educational institutions controlled at the state level, the percentages of the SC and the ST renewed seats are fixed in accordance to their population in the state population. A few states also had percentage of seats reserved for the OBCs. The Mandal Commission had recommended reservation for 27 per cent of the OBC in the educational institutions and employment. HRD Minister, Arjun Singh introduced 27 per cent reservation for OBC in private aided and unaided educational institutions and deemed universities.

The reservation for the SCs and the STs in more or less an established fact. Various arguments are put forth for supporting the Scheduled Castes and the Scheduled Tribes reservations are:

(1) The Constitution of India mentions the right to reserved seats to them.

(2) These communities have been subject to grave injustices and discrimination for centuries in the case of the SCs or have remained isolated in the case of the STs and reservations are a measure of compensatory justice which is instrumental in helping these communities to move up the social and economic ladder.

(3) The 'systematic discrimination' has rendered them incapable to compete on the basis of 'merit'.

(4) The benefit which they derive from reservations is at the entry level and have to meet the same syllabus and standards as the others who are pursuing the similar degree.

(5) They overcome all difficulties and gain entry at a top level medical college, which is due to their hard work and intellectual ability.

The reservations for the SCs and STs have evidently opened more doors for the demand of OBCs in various spheres, i.e., in educational institutions, in public employment and in representative legislative assemblies. Although the OBCs did not suffer the oppression of caste system, untouchability or exclusion to the extent of SCs and STs, but have received a systematic disadvantage in accessing education and middle class jobs. This reiterates the fact that OBCs have been subjected to unequal opportunities and differences in the society, necessitating governmental action. According to the National Sample Survey, of every 1000 upper caste Hindu in urban areas in India, 253 were graduates while, among the Hindu OBCs there are only 86 graduates per 1000. This number sharply dips when we see the figure at the post graduate level or the professional degrees. The controversy over reservations policies in India has resulted from reservations of OBCs in the admissions to educational institutions and in the public employment.

The first Amendment of the Indian Constitution in 1951 under Article 15(4) empowered the state to make any "special provision for the advancement of any socially and educationally backward classes of citizens or for the SCs and STs." The first Backward Classes Commission headed by the Kaka Kalelkar was found which "enumerated approximately 1,200 OBCs based on social and economic criteria which did not have a major impact."

The Mandal Commission was appointed in 1978 by the Morarji Desai Government, which catered to the consideration of affirmative action policies for the backward and disadvantaged castes. The Commission submitted its report in December, 1980 recommending the existing reservations of OBCs upto 27 per cent for all services including public sector undertakings under the Central Government and 27 per cent of all admissions to institutions of higher education except in the states that have reserved higher percentages for the OBCs.

The Mandal Commission has claimed that the OBCs were 52.1 per cent of the India's population and recommended 27 per cent reservations for them.

The simple mathematical logic of 27 per cent OBC reservation is derived from the fact that Supreme Court has capped the upper limit of quotas at 50 per cent. The SCs and the STs are already getting 22.5 per cent reservations and the maximum quota for the OBC is 27 per cent. So, the figure of 27 per cent has nothing to do with the population estimate.

In August 1990, Prime Minister, V.P. Singh announced implementation of the recommendations of the Mandal Commission in the case of government jobs. This announced a set of virulent protests and self-immolations on the streets, especially in northern regions of India.

The National Commission for Backward Classes (NCBC) constituted in the wake of Mandal Commission explained on the statutory premise that "identification of backwardness is an ever-continuing process of inclusion and exclusion." But all recommendations have been in favour of including more castes in the OBC category while its power to recommend "exclusion of those who do not qualify" has remained a dead letter. The number of centrally notified OBC has risen from 1,257 castes in 1993 to 2,297 in the year 2006.

One of the oddaties of the Central List is that the tiny Union Territory of Pondicherry has contributed 262 castes, while the largest state in terms of area, Rajasthan, has only 65 castes.

The United Progressive Alliance government in the month of April, 2006 proposed to introduce 27 per cent reservations for the OBCs in the higher education sector, both public and private. The proposed legislation had provisions that gave government unprecedented power not only to impose quotas in over 100 "deemed universities" and over and about 32 Central Universities but also aimed to regulate their fees selection procedure and even take punitive action.

The provisions of the Bill, titled as Central Educational Institutions (Reservations of Seats and Regulation of Admission and Fee) Bill, 2006, are:

Quotas specified: 15 for SCs; 7.5 for STs and 27 for OBCs.

New names in this quota net: Institutions, aided and unaided by the Government, and deemed to be universities will now be "Central educational institutions" to which the above percentages will apply.

UGC decides: The University Grants Commission will have the power to regulate admissions and fees in these institutions.

Two fee packages: There will be a "differential fee structure" for SC/ST/OBC students to make "reservation a meaningful reality." The Centre can specify what the difference in few should be.

Mandatory increase in seats: The Government can, "by order, direct any Central Educational Institution to increase the number of seats in each branch or faculty," to protect the number of seats available for general students. In other words, no IIT or IIM can refuse to increase seats.

Say in selection: Unaided institutions deemed to be universities shall make admissions in "a fair and transparent manner," on the basis of qualifying examinations prescribed by UGC.

Monitoring: The Centre has power to check for compliance with the provisions by the institutions.

Punitive action: In case of violation, the Centre can withhold grants, withdraw deemed university status, take "any other appropriate action under relevant acts."

THE ISSUE OF STATISTICS OF OBCS

According to 2001 census, out of India's population of 1,028,737,436 the Scheduled Castes comprises 166,635,700 and Scheduled Tribe 84,326,240, that is 16.2 per cent and 8.2 per cent respectively. There is no data on OBCs in the census. However, according to National Sample Survey's 1999-2000 round, around 36 per cent of the country's population is defined as belonging to the Other Backward Classes (OBC). The proportion falls to 32 per cent on excluding Muslim OBCs. A survey conducted in 1998 by National Family Health Statistics (NFHS) puts the proportion of non-Muslim OBCs as 29.8 per cent.

Around 36 per cent of the country's population is defined as belonging to the Other Backward Classes according to the National Sample Survey's 1999-2000 round, and not 52 per cent as defined by the Mandal Commission, a number that most politicians still use while asking for reservation.

If we are to exclude Muslim OBCs, the proportion falls to 32 per cent according to the NSS, 1999-2000. Indeed, Yogendra Yadav, Professor at the Delhi-based Centre for the Study of Developing Societies, who is in favour of reservation for OBCs, agrees that there is no empirical basis to the Mandal figure: "It is a mythical construct based on reducing the number of SC/ST, Muslims and others and then arriving at a number." Regarding the estimate of OBC population he further comments, "this figure was based on back-of-envelope calculation by remainder method and has not been backed by any social scientific evidence. The NSS has put the figure at 36 per cent, but this is based on 'self-reporting' and likely to underestimate the OBC population. The most robust estimate is anywhere between 40 to 44 per cent. We can't have more precise information because the census does not collect information about the OBC population."

One of the reasons for the much higher Mandal number is that it defined OBCs in socioeconomic terms, and so included, for instance, "castes/classes considered as socially backward by others." If, to cite another of the 11 criteria used, the percentage of married women below 17 years is a fourth above the state's average in rural areas (and 10 per cent in urban areas), the community is considered to be OBC.

Similarly, if castes/classes where the proportion of working women is 25 per cent higher than the state's average, the castes/classes are considered OBC—today's double-income families, if living in areas where women do not work, would then be considered OBCs using the Mandal definition.

In the NSS case, respondents were asked to indicate their caste, and this was then tallied with the list of castes that each state defines as OBC. The NSS data is also corroborated by the National Family Health Statistics, a survey conducted in 1998 by the DHS, which has conducted 200 such surveys in 75 countries. The NFHS data show that the proportion of non-Muslim OBCs is 29.8 per cent, a figure quite close to the NSS' 32.1 per cent. For SC/ST, while the NSS shows this is 28.3 per cent of the population, the NFHS estimates this at 27.9 per cent. The 2001 Census estimated the SC/ST population at 24.4 per cent, though the Census did not cover any information on OBCs.

The share of the Muslims (including OBC Muslims) in all three data sets is quite similar, ranging from 11 to 13 per cent. So far, the Supreme Court ceiling of 50 per cent on all reservations has been justified by arguing this covers only the non-creamy layer OBCs, since 22.5 per cent of all reservations are for SC/ST, leaving 27.5 per cent for the OBCs that is, only around half the OBCs would be entitled to reservations.

If, we use the NSS/NFHS figures, a 50 per cent reservation ceiling will cover three fourths of all OBCs, and if Muslim OBCs are to be kept out of reservations, then 86 per cent of the remaining will get covered by reservations.

IS THE 104th AMENDMENT BILL DANGEROUS?

T.R. Andhy Arjuna questioning the timings that caused the government to make this move to introduce reservations, says, "Even after the Mandal judgment of the Supreme Court in 1992, which gave the go ahead for 27 per cent reservations of OBCs in public services for over 14 years, the Central Government did not think of OBC reservations until Arjun Singh's sudden announcement in April." Before this move, the government had passed the 93rd Constitutional Amendment Act in December, 2005, originally drafted as

104th Amendment Bill in order to pave way for such a reservation scheme.

The 104th Constitution Amendment Bill, provides reservations for the socially and educationally backward classes, besides the Scheduled Classes and Scheduled Tribes, in all private aided and unaided educational institutions. The amendment is the government's attempt to offset the effect of the recent Supreme Court judgment that categorically said that in an unaided (which runs without government funding) educational institution—whether run by non-minorities or minorities—the government cannot implement its policy of reservation. "*This* amendment is nothing short of a revolution because good education is every Indian *family's dream*," Indira Jaising, state eminent Constitution expert said. "For the first time, unaided private institutions — where better education is provided — are now under the purview of the State. Private education institutions that are accruing huge profits and no responsibilities felt no obligation to Dalits. This is no longer the case," Jaisingh added.

The political mileage resulting from the move, which directly benefits more than 70 per cent of voters, is so huge that of the 381 members present in the Lok Sabha, 379 voted in favour of it. The important amendment is an attempt by Congress to re-establish its lost credentials among tribals, Dalits and Other Backward Classes who have moved away from it since the emergence of regional parties and the Bharatiya Janata Party.

It is important to analyse the repercussions arising out of this amendment. According to Amulya Ganguli, the trouble arises when a political party eyes a vote bank, it forgets that other too are on the prowl. The BJP can't stomach the huge chunk of the vote bank going Congress' way. It somewhat convincingly asked why minority-managed—meaning Christian and Muslim—institutions are not included in the amendment. The BJP wants substantial reservation for socially and educationally backward castes in these minority institutions also. Minority institutions have staunchly resisted the move.

Although Article 30 of the Indian Constitution provides the right to minorities to establish and administer educational institutions, in practice they have become highly commercialised where poor or backward students can't even dream of getting education. For instance, in Andhra Pradesh there are 9,000 engineering seats in minority colleges which were not filled up because they could not find students rich enough to pay for them. The Bill is certainly going to upset upper-caste Hindus because it will shrink seats in the general category. The BJP attempts to capitalise on both these classes' sentiments be unsuccessfully moving an amendment to the Bill to get Muslim and Christian educational institutions under the purview of the Bill. The BJP's Ananth Kumar argued in Parliament that, 'I do not know why the UPA *[United Progressive Alliance]* government has not given this provision of reservation to the minority institutions. This Constitutional Amendment is an eyewash. 'After passing this lopsided Constitution (Amendment) Bill there would be no medical colleges, no engineering colleges, no IT institutions, no Law institutions in 2006, 2007, 2008 and 2009 in the name of non-minority institutions,' he argued. Hence, the BJP had protested that minority education institutions should also come under the purview of the Bill, but did not effect the Bill in principle. The 104th Constitution Amendment Bill was passed in the Lok Sabha with 379 votes in favour and one vote against and one abstaining. The Rajya Sabha also passed it with 172 votes in favour and only two against.

The 104th Constitution Amendment Bill became the Constitution 93rd Amendment Act, 2005 when President Kalam signed it on January 20, 2006 after coming very close to withholding his assent to the Bill. President Kalam had raised a number of queries and Prime Minister Manmohan Singh was apparently able to address all queries to the President's satisfaction.

TIME FOR RESERVATION IN MINORITY INSTITUTIONS

'The UP A government is doing a draconian social injustice and creating a minority private institutions bazaar in the country. Education should not be nationalised and education should also be in the private domain.' In reality, the minority-run institutions have not been above board. During the debate, politicians cited an example that in Mumbai, more than 70 per cent of the majority-run institutions claim a minority status.

BJP leader, Bal Apte, in the Rajya Sabha argued, 'The main problem is not of religious minorities, but of linguistic minorities. They hardly have the presence of their community in a particular region, but because their language is different, they establish an institution and claim a minority status and that really gives them an opportunity to earn money.'

All over India, minorities do run a few exceptionally dedicated institutions, helping the poor and bringing social justice, but most of them are profit-making machines. The demand to include minority institutions are raised loudly because the private institutions are better managed than the government-owned institutions. In Karnataka, at least four government colleges do not have even 60 per cent of the required staff. There is shortage of 20 to 30 per cent in premier higher and technical education institutions. It is estimated that nearly Rs 450 billion is spent for professional courses, including medical, dental and engineering, in India. The hidden question is whether education is a business, trade or a national mission and an instrument to bring social justice.

According to R.L. Jalappa of the Congress, "Around 85,000 seats were vacant in the engineering stream during the year 2003-04 in India. In Karnataka state alone, 400 seats in dental colleges were not filled up. It was very difficult for us to fill up the seats in the dental as well as for the MBBS courses. Now, the government is proposing to bring about reservation. Who will foot the bill for the tuition fees?"

The political issue of reservation in educational institution is so important, fundamental and explosive that every time it comes up for debate politicians get into their act. While passing the law, politicians ask for more by arguing why there is a need to have reservations in the judiciary and the bureaucracy. Out of about 100 secretary-level officers, not even one is a Scheduled Caste, they complained.

There are approximately 16 to 20 million Dalit Christians who have been denied reservation. Already, a powerful section of the government, including Prime Minister Manmohan Singh and Congress Chief Sonia Gandhi, are contemplating reservation in jobs in the private sector. Many MPs cutting across party lines argued that there should be reservation for the economically backward. One of the MP said, "A person who migrates from one state to another should be provided reservation in that state also."

Like it happens in the case of most issues, opinions got vertically divided when the House passed the bill. It is now being argued that a new kind of reservation will pit Muslims and Christians against Dalits and Tribals. Dr. Udit Raj, Chairman, All India Confederation of SC/ST Organisations, says, "I am happy that the Bill has been passed but we wanted to include the minority institutions. But the Congress is indulging in appeasement of minorities. There is a truth that the Congress party appeases minorities more than it really gives them something."

Maneka Gandhi, MP from Uttar Pradesh, said, "The government is manufacturing fertile ground to sow, nurture and harvest the evils of separatism, keep people divided on religious grounds. The present attempt is not only short-sighted but antithetical to any hopes of narrowing India's religious divisions. By keeping religious segregations alive, the government is going against the very purpose of the inception of these institutions."

Human Resource Development Minister Arjun Singh, who moved the Bill, could not hide his glee when he replied to the BJP on why minority institutions cannot be included. 'Minority rights, as specified in Article 30, should, in all circumstances, be protected. This Article has a great historical necessity.

Therefore, it cannot be deleted.' He also said, "In the light of the trauma of Partition, Article 30 was put into our Constitution as a Fundamental Right because this country, this republic, gave the assurances to these people that they will not be discriminated against and that they will be protected, and, therefore, it was better for them to stay where they were."

IMPLICATIONS OF THE 93RD CONSTITUTION AMENDMENT ACT

The 93rd Constitution Amendment Act was "enacted by Parliament for a totally different purpose i.e. to overcome the 12th August, 2005 decision of the Supreme Court in the *Inamdar Case*." The Supreme Court delivered an unanimous judgement by seven judges on 12 August, 2005 in the case of *P.A. Inamdar and Ors vs. State of Maharashtra and Ors.* declaring that the state can't impose its reservation policy on minority and non-minority unaided private colleges, including professional colleges. "In that case the apex court had struck down the existing reservations made by the state governments in private unaided medical and engineering institutions, because it held that such institutions had a fundamental right to occupation guaranteed by Article 19, Clause 1(g) of the Constitution and the states did not have the power to impose such reservations on them. Prior to the Inamdar case, several states had for over 15 to 20 years made reservations in private unaided professional institutions for SCs and STs and OBCs. The *Inamdar* case for the first time, declared these reservations illegal. Thus, the 93rd Amendment had a very limited objective to restore the status quo ante to the *Inamdar's* case and enable the states to make reservations even in private unaided educational institutions." All political parties without exception were unhappy with the Supreme Court's recent judgement in the P.A. Inamdar case and there was a consensus among all political parties for amending the Constitution to impose the State's reservation policies on the private unaided colleges too, the Government reacted very quickly.

According to the Constitution 93rd Amendment Act, 2005,

> Amendment of Article 15.—In Article 15 of the Constitution, after clause (4), the following clause shall be inserted, namely: (5) Nothing in this article or in sub-clause (g) of clause (1) of article 19 shall prevent the State from making any special provision, by law, for the advancement of any socially and educationally backward classes of citizens or for the Scheduled Castes or the Scheduled Tribes in so far as such special provisions relate to their admission to educational institutions including private educational institutions, whether aided or unaided by the State, other than the minority educational institutions referred to in clause (1) of article 30. It declared that nothing in the Fundamental Rights of a private educational institutions can prevent making such reservations.

While the Amendment was clearly intended to bring all private institutions, whether aided or unaided, under the purview of the Government's policies on reservation and fee structure, it has also quietly achieved much more than that by widening the scope of the Amendment Act to specifically include the term "admission to educational institutions." Article 15 of the Constitution, as it was originally framed in 1950, stated the following and did not include the term "admission to educational institutions."

The operational part of the Bill in section 2, under reservation of seats in educational institution for SCs, STs and OBCs reservation in respect of the annual permitted strength in each branch or faculty for admission into educational institutions. . . may be prescribed subject to a maximum of 50 per cent of all seats in each such branch or faculty. "Section 4 mentions that the central government will notify rules to carry out the purpose of this act."

The draft defines educational institution as set up under an Act of Parliament which shall include Central Universities, Institutions of National importance and institutions deemed to be universities, any educational institution established under law by the central government whether maintained by it or otherwise and "all other aided/unaided institutions affiliated, to the first category." So, the term "educational institutions" could be interpreted by the current or any future government to include all schools from nursery schools or institutions like NIITs or others offering specialised training.

ANTI-QUOTA STIR

Following the government's announcement to implement 27 per cent reservation for OBCs in the institutions of higher learning, there were sharp reactions from the student communities in the institutes concerned especially the upper caste metropolitan medical graduates from medical institutes, and also, opposition from the students of other colleges not getting affected by the proposed reservation scheme. Students gathered under the banner of "Youth for Equality" and demanded that the government should roll back its decision to grant more reservations. In north India it led to protests, including hunger strikes especially by medical students though the government and the police took stern measures to suppress the protestors.

Describing the agitation of medical students, B.K. Roy Burman said, "The medico had launched a holy war with crusader zeal against this reservation policy of the government. The leaders of their organization had given a call to the campeers to rush to Delhi and join the protest activities. They argued that any further reservations would completely disrupt the meritarian principle of admission to institutions of higher learning. The medical students also attempted self-immolation in a few cases."

On 28th April, 2006, Human Resource Development Minister, Arjun Singh apologised to the students who were protesting outside his office in New Delhi, and were manhandled by the security officers there. However, he refused to offer any assurance that he would seriously reconsider his proposal which he has submitted to the union cabinet of reserving 27 per cent of seats in premier educational institutions across India for the caste subgroups labelled as 'other backward castes'. Mr. Singh has been under pressure for the students were protesting across the country, intellectuals were slamming his proposal as compartmentalisation of India, and the Election Commission was accusing him of violating the "model code" by announcing such populist measures right before assembly elections were due in five states across India. However, with the OBCs comprising of 52 per cent of India's electorate, none of the main political parties could vociferously oppose the scheme.

In Mumbai on 17 May, 2006, the police beat the peaceful anti-reservation agitators (medical students of King Edward and other medical colleges of Mumbai) with sticks, leading to a furor among the other students in the other cities. Pro-reservation groups have claimed the anti-reservation protests have succeeded largely due to biased media reporting.

Two members of the National Knowledge Commission- Dr. P.B. Mehta and Dr. Andre Beteille resigned opposing the reservation move. Dr. P.B. Mehta and Dr. Andre Beteille made their positions clear in the resignation letters which they made public.

The Indian Express carried resignation letter of Pradap Bhanu Mehta in which he wrote:

"These measures will not achieve social justice. I am as committed as anyone to two propositions. Every student must be enabled to realise his/her full potential regardless of financial or social circumstances. Achieving this aim requires medical forms of affirmative action. But the numerically mandated quoted your government is proposing are deeply disappointing.

As a society we focus on reservations largely because it is a way of avoiding doing the things that really create access. Increasing the supply of goods, quality institutions at all levels (not to be confused with numerical increases), more robust scholarship and support programmes will go much further than numerically mandated quotas. When you assumed office you had sketched out a vision of combining economic reform with social justice. Increased public investment is going to be central to creating access opportunities. It would be presumptuous for me to suggest where this increased public investment is going to come from, but there are ample possibilities, for instance, earmarking proceeds from genuine disinvestments for education will do far more for access than quotas. We are not doing enough to genuinely empower marginalized groups, but are offering condescending palliatives like quotas as substitute. All the measures-currently under discussion are to defuse the agitation, not to lay the foundations for a vibrant education system. If I may borrow a phrase of Tom Paine's, we pity the plumage, but forget the dying bird."

Apprehending that the agitation against the quotas would become as intense as it was during the anti-Mandal agitation in 1990, on 15 May, 2006, the Centre declared to come out with a "mechanism" on the reservations issue protecting the interests of all sections of the society. The announcement did not have a positive impact and the protestors continued with anti-quota stir. On 17 May, 2006, the government announced to constitutionally informed committee comprising of three Union Ministers namely Defence Minister Pranab Mukherjee, HRD Minister Arjun Singh and Finance Minister P. Chidambaram, to be instrumental in evolving the "mechanism" to set out the reservations issue after considering the various view points from different segments of the society.

Yet, the medical students were not ready to give up their stir against the caste based reservation to the OBCs in the higher education. The stir was joined by the students of other "affected" centrally funded educational institutions like the IITs, IIMs and other medical institutions. The agitating doctors and medical students responded to the Supreme Court's direction, while the Prime Minister's appeal to the striking students had failed.

SUPREME COURT INTERVENES IN RESERVATIONS ISSUE

Litigation is perhaps an option that the doctors striking against the reservation policy would have preferred to avoid. When the Supreme Court Vacation Bench advised them to suspend their agitation as the court was set to hear some petitions challenging the validity of the policy, they were in no mood to listen. The Bench, therefore, issued an order on 31st May, 2006 directing them to resume work.

Although the court did not threaten the striking doctors with punitive action if they violated its directive, the prospect of such action forced most of the agitating doctors to fall in line. In the process, counsel appearing for the agitating doctors managed to secure two extraordinary concessions from the Bench. First, the Bench directed that in case the protests were called off, the government should not take any punitive action. Second, if the services of any doctor has been terminated for participating in the strike, the government should permit them to join duty.

There were two petitions before the Supreme Court Bench, one by Ashoka Kumar Thakur, an advocate, who questioned the basis of reservation, and the second by Shiv Khera, who challenged the validity of the Constitutional 93rd Amendment inserting Article 15(5) as an enabling provision to introduce reservation for OBCs. The Resident Doctors Association of Maulana Azad Medical College and the All India Institute of Medical Sciences, New Delhi, have filed an interlocutory application, in which they challenged the entire reservation policy followed since 1950, alleging that there was no data to support the policy. They also questioned the government's reliance on the Mandal Commission report, without fulfilling its requirement that social and economic conditions be reviewed periodically before extending reservation. The Bench refused to restrain the government from implementing the reservation policy, but held that if it implemented it, it would be subject to the outcome of the case before it. The Bench, comprising Justices Arijit Pasayat and Lokeshwar Singh Panta, framed the basic issues in the petitions before them as follows; What is the basis for the determination/classification as to who belongs to the OBCs and the modalities to be adopted for the implementation of the policy in question. It directed that in' the counter-affidavit to be filed by the government and other respondents, these aspects shall be dealt with.

The Supreme Court observed that the proposed 27 per cent OBC quota in all Central educational institutions is capable of dividing this great nation on caste basis and issued notices on 28 May, 2006 to the Centre and six ministers asking them to answer what was the "rationale" behind the classification of a class of citizens as "OBC."

On the hearings on PIL, a vacation bench of Justice Arijit Pasayat and Justice Lokeshwar Singh Panta made it clear tnat "as a matter of fact it (the case) requires judicial review" and asked the Union of India to answer three crucial questions:

(i) What is the basis of norms for fixing the OBC category?

(ii) What is the rational behind fixing it?

(iii) If the proposed reservation is implemented, what are the modalities and basis for modalities?

"These question has serious and sensitive social and political ramifications and if the necessity so arises, the issue shall be dealt with appropriately when the matter is taken up for final hearing," it said. The court sought counter affidavit within eight weeks from the concerned Ministries like Social Justice and Empowerment, Human Resource Development, Science and Technology, Commerce, Health and Department of Statistics and Programme on the Petitions.

However, it appears that the petitioners have ignored the justification for reservation in the judgment in *Indra Sawhney vs. Union of India* in 1993. Although it was with reference to the implementation of the Mandal Commission recommendations, to ensure adequate representation of OBCs in Central services, the principles laid down by the Court would certainly apply to reservation in educational institutions as well.

The petitioners apparently argue that caste is not the proper basis to determine who belongs to OBCs, as it is inherently divisive. It is worth quoting the Courts judgement in the Indra Sawhney case (paragraph 83): "Any authority entrusted with the task of identifying backward classes may well start with the castes. . . . Since caste represents an existing, identifiable social group spread over an overwhelming majority of the country's population, we say one may well begin with castes, if one so chooses, and then go to other groups, sections and classes. If the real object is to discover and locate backwardness, and if such backwardness is found in caste it can be treated as backward; if it is found in any other group, section or class, they too can be treated as backward." It observed in paragraph 85:"[The] Mandal Commission appointed under Article 340 was concerned only with the socially and educational backward classes contemplated by the said Article. Even so, it is evident that social backwardness has been given procedure over other by the Mandal Commission-12 out of 22 total points social backwardness—it may be reiterated—leads to educational and economic backwardness. No objection can be, none is taken, to the validity and relevancy of the criteria adopted by the Mandal Commission."

It further said,

> "The criteria evolved by Mandal Commission for defining identifying the OBCs cannot be said to be irrelevant. May be there are certain errors on actual exercise of identification in the nature of over inclusion or under-inclusion, as the case may be. But in an exercise of such magnitude and complexity, such errors are not uncommon. These errors cannot be made a basis for rejecting either the relevance of the criteria evolved by the Commission or the entire exercise of identification."

The Court pointed out that the Office Memorandum issued by the V.P. Singh government implementing 27 per cent reservation in Central services on August 13, 1990, did not incorporate the Mandal Lists of OBCs as such. It incorporates in truth and effect the State Lists (as only those common to both the lists were included). As the Centre's move to extend 27 per cent reservation for OBCs in educational institutions in criticised on the grounds that it is based on wrong data, these observations of the Supreme Court are relevant. If the Centre adopts the same list of OBCs applicable in the Central services for use in educational institutions, it cannot be assailed as invalid.

The protesters who have expressed lack of faith in the Executive in implementing the reservation policy may well ponder over what the Court had said in this case: "In a social measure like the impugned one, the Court must give due regard to the judgement of the Executive, a co-equal wing of the state, and approach the measure in the spirit in which it is conceived."

MANDAL REVISITED

The second Backward Class Commission or the Mandal Commission, known popularly so after its Chairman Bindeshwari Prasad Mandal, is a watershed in the history of independent India. Since December 1980, when the Mandal Commission submitted its report, life for Indian youth has changed dramatically. To comprehend the profound impact it has had on the lives of one and all, we must first understand the genesis of the reservation policy in India.

Reservation policy in India has been viewed as an effort by the Constitution framers for the advancement of the socially and the educationally backward classes of India. The policy as such is creditable, especially if it is associated with a periodic review, in this case ten years. However, in India the basis of reservation was caste. It soon became a tool in the hands of unscrupulous and opportunist politicians, who even after sixty years of independence are playing the caste card to inflate their vote bank and check their declining political stature.

India is divided into many endogamous groups, or castes and sub-castes, as a result of centuries of practicing a form of social hierarchy called the caste system. The traditional caste system was divided into four main varnas, Shudras being the lowest in the social hierarchy. The majority of the communities classified as 'Other Backward Classes' or the OBCs belonged to the Shudra varna in the traditional social hierarchy but were however, superior to the out castes or the untouchables. Most of the communities included under the OBCs are basically occupation castes - Lohar, Sonar, Darzi, Badhai, Teli, etc. These lower castes have undoubtedly been discriminated against by the so called upper castes in the social hierarchy, for thousands of years.

Before independence efforts were started for the advancement of the lower castes and the minority groups, with the aim of undoing centuries of oppression and discrimination. In 1909, the Morley-Minto reforms introduced communal electorates for the first time in India, by reserving seats to Indian Muslims in the legislature, but not for the lower castes. The Simon Commission in 1927, recommended reservation of seats for the lower castes in the legislative council, to enhance their political stature by giving them representation. This was regarded as a tentative measure to augment the conditions of the lower castes. In 1932, the British Government introduced the Poona Pact or the Communal Award, which granted separate seats to the 'Depressed Classes' in the Provincial Assemblies and the right of double vote under which they were to elect their own representatives and to vote also in the general constituencies. This again was supposed to be a temporary measure but this went on to be incorporated into the Government of India Act of 1935. This act for the first time introduced the term 'Scheduled Castes' which was then a list of castes, races and tribes which were considered as lower castes as mentioned in the 1931 caste census. In 1942, B.R. Ambedkar put forth the demand for reservations for the Scheduled castes in government services and education. When India attained independence in 1947, Ambedkar was appointed as the Chairman of the Drafting Committee for the Indian Constitution.

The Constitution of India which came into effect from 26 January, 1950, included safeguards for depressed and Other Backward Classes. Though the Indian Constitution prohibits any discrimination based on religion, race, caste, sex and place of birth, the Constitution also contains special clauses to ensure reservation, "for the advancement of any socially and educationally backward classes of citizens." Under the Constitution of India, 15 per cent of educational and civil service seats were reserved for "Scheduled Castes" and 7.5 per cent for "Scheduled Tribes." Besides making special provisions for the Scheduled Castes and tribes, the Constitution made separate provisions for the amelioration and advancement of the 'backward classes'. It made provisions for the appointment of a 'Commission to investigate the conditions of backward classes' under Article 340. Besides in 1951 an amendment to the Constitution stated that the State can make special provisions for advancement of any backward class. Keeping the provisions of Article 340 in mind, a Commission was appointed on January 29, 1953 with Kaka Saheb Kalelkar as Chairman. Its primary objective was to determine the criterion by which any particular class or group of people can be called 'backward'. It was asked to prepare a list of such backward communities for the whole of India and to recommend measures to be taken for their amelioration. The commission submitted its report on 30 March, 1955. It had prepared a list of 2,399 backward castes or communities for the entire country and of which 837 had been classified as the "most backward." Some of the most notable recommendations of the commission were:

1. Undertaking caste-wise enumeration of population in the census of 1961;
2. Relating social backwardness of a class to its low position in the traditional caste hierarchy of Hindu society;
3. Treating all women as a class as "backward";

4. Reservation of 70 per cent seats in all technical and professional institutions for qualified students of backward classes;
5. Reservation of vacancies in all government services and local bodies for Other Backward Classes;
6. It recommended "caste as the criteria" to determine backwardness.

The Government found its recommendations to be vague and unpractical and hence did not implement the same. However, the State Governments were authorised to make provisions for the backward classes according to the lists prepared by state governments themselves. Another landmark in that, history of reservation policy in India was the Supreme Court mandate of 1963 that the reservations in any institution could not exceed 50 per cent.

The decision to set up a second Backward Class Commission was taken in 1978 by Morarji Desai Government. This was officially announced on January 1, 1979 and, Indian Parliamentarian Bindeshwari Prasad Mandal was appointed its Chairman. The main objective of the Commission was to assess the present situation of the backward classes and recommend the steps for their advancement and redress caste discrimination going on in the society. Since the figures of caste wise population are not available beyond 1931, the Commission used the 1931 census data to calculate the number of OBCs. To identify the OBCs, the Mandal Commission adopted various methods and techniques to gather the essential data and evidence.

The Mandal Commission adopted various methods and techniques to collect the necessary data and evidence. The commission evolved eleven criteria which under three major headings: social, educational and economic in order to identify OBCs.

SOCIAL

1. Castes/classes considered as socially backward by others.

2. Castes/classes which mainly depend on manual labour for their livelihood.
3. Castes/classes where at least 25 per cent females and 10 per cent males above the state average get married at an age below 17 years in rural areas and at least 10 per cent females and 5 per cent males do so in urban areas.
4. Castes/classes where participation of females in work is at least 25 per cent above the state average.

EDUCATIONAL

1. Castes/classes where the number of children in the age group of 5-15 years who never attended school is at least 25 per cent above the state average.
2. Castes/classes where the rate of student drop-out in the age group of 5-15 years is at least 25 per cent above the state average.
3. Castes/classes amongst whom the proportion of matriculates is at least 25 per cent below the state average.

ECONOMIC

1. Castes/classes where the average value of family assets is at least 25 per cent below the state average.
2. Castes/classes where the number of families living in kuccha houses is at least 25 per cent above the state average.
3. Castes/classes where the source of drinking water is beyond half a kilometer for more than 50 per cent of the households.
4. Castes/classes where the number of households having taken consumption loans is at least 25 per cent above the state average.

WEIGHTAGE

A separate weightage was given to all these criteria i.e. three each were given to form social indicators, two point to each of points three educational indicators and one point to each of the four economic indicators. A score of 11 points or more of the total of 22 points were considered necessary for listing castes/classes as socially and educationally backward. All castes which had a score of 50 per cent or above by applying the score were listed a socially and educationally backward and the rest were treated as "advanced."

The Commission identified 54 per cent of the total population (excluding SCs and STs) as backward and further classified 1257 communities under this category. The Commission submitted its report in December 1980. The observations of the Commission were that, "The population of OBCs which includes both Hindus and non-Hindus is around 52 per cent of the total population. However, only 27 per cent of reservation was recommended owing to the legal constraint that the total quantum of reservation should not exceed 50 per cent (these 27 per cent in fact were in addition to the 15 per cent in favour of the Scheduled Castes and the 7.5 per cent in favour of the Scheduled Tribes)." The authors of the report justified their recommendations in new terms:

> 'It is not at all our contention that by offering a few thousands jobs to OBC candidates we shall be able to make 52 per cent of the Indian population as forward. But we must recognise that an essential part of the battle against social backwardness is to be fought in the minds of the backward people. In India, government service has always been looked upon as a symbol of prestige and power. By increasing the representation of OBCs in government services, we *give them an immediate feeling of participation in the governance of this country*. When a backward class candidate becomes a Collector or a Superintendent of Police, the material benefits accruing from his position are limited to the members of his family

only. But the psychological spin off of this phenomenon is tremendous; the entire community of that backward class candidate feels socially elevated. Even when no tangible benefits flow to the community at large, the feeling that now it has its 'own man' in the 'corridors of power' acts as morale booster.'

States which have already introduced reservation for OBC exceeding 27 per cent were not be affected by this recommendation. With this general recommendation the commission proposed the following overall scheme of reservation for OBC:

1. Candidates belonging to OBC recruited on the basis of merit in an open competition should not be adjusted against their reservation quota of 27 per cent.
2. The above reservation should also be made applicable to promotion quota at all levels.
3. Reserved quota remaining unfilled should be carried forward for a period of three years and de-reserved thereafter.
4. Relaxation in the upper age limit for direct recruitment should be extended to the candidates of OBC in the same manner as done in the case of SCs and STs.
5. A roster system for each category of posts should be adopted by the concerned authorities in the same manner as presently done in respect of SC and ST candidates.

These recommendations in total are applicable to all recruitment to public sector undertakings both under the central and state governments, as also to nationalised banks. All private sector undertakings which have received financial assistance from the government in one form or other should also be obliged to recruit personnel on the aforesaid basis. All universities and affiliated colleges should also be covered by the above scheme of reservation. Although education is considered an important factor to bring a desired social change, "educational reform" was not within the terms of reference of this commission. To promote literacy the following measures were suggested:

1. An intensive time-bound programme for adult education should be launched in selected pockets with high concentration of OBC population;
2. Residential schools should be set up in these areas for backward class students to provide a climate specially conducive to serious studies. All facilities in these schools including boarding and lodging should be provided free of cost to attract students from poor and backward homes;
3. Separate hostels for OBC students with above facilities will have to be provided;
4. Vocational training was considered imperative;
5. It was recommended that seats should be reserved for OBC students in all scientific, technical and professional institutions run by the central as well as state governments. The quantum of reservation should be the same as in the government services, i.e., 27 per cent.

The implementation of Mandal Commission recommendations led to nationwide protests and great deal of controversy. The criticism was sharp and colleges across the country held massive protests against it. Soon after, Rajiv Goswami student of Delhi University, self-immolated himself in protest of the government's actions. His act further sparked a series of self-immolations by other college students and led to a formidable movement against job reservations for Backward Castes in India. It finally resulted in the resignation of the then Prime Minister V.P. Singh.

It was popularly argued that it is unfair to accord people special privileges on the basis of caste, even in order to redress traditional caste discrimination. This was primarily because allocating quotas on the basis of caste is a form of racial discrimination which is contrary to the right to equality and is contrary to the spirit of the Constitution. Such a reservation policy may consequently lead to legislations for providing reservation for other religious minorities like Christians and Muslims in all government education institutions. Such a discrimination on the basis of religion is contrary to the ideas of secularism. It is also feared that the economically well off people of the so called backward castes would corner all the benefits of reservation. Besides, even among OBCs, the upper OBCs like the Yadavs, Kurmis, Jats, etc. were relatively more powerful than the lower OBCs or the OBCs like the Kanhars, Noniyas, Telis, etc. would effectively corner the benefits of reservation policy. L.R. Nayak, a member of the Mandal Commission, foresaw this 25 years back and refused to sign the Mandal Report. The astronomical rise in the powers of Yadavs, Jats, etc. is a glaring example of the sound reason behind anti-Mandal protests.

The protestors also argued that the quality of the elite institutions may go down. Also without improving primary and secondary education, it makes no sense reserving seats for the higher education. It was very obvious to one and all that the politicians were trying to divide people on the basis of caste to favour their own vote bank. This way the politicians were only perpetuating the evil caste system and throwing, a rising democracy backwards into the dark ages. Reservation policy was viewed as a big letdown for the meritorious and deserving students. It was also feared that this policy would increase the phenomenon of Brain Drain from India. Even the undergraduates and graduates will start moving to foreign universities for higher education. Today, the percentage of students aspiring to study abroad has increased manifold as a result of a 'quota politics'. Also it was feared that reservation policy would be a big setback for privatisation in India and would deviate the Multinational Corporations from investing in India. The memorandum issued on 25 September, 1991, by the Narasimha Rao Government carried a second notification specifying that (a) within the 27 percent, reservations preference should be given to candidates belonging to the poorer sections of the backward castes, and (b) an additional 10 per cent of the vacancies should be reserved for the economically backward classes of the people. No criteria, however, were issued for determining the poorer sections of the other economically backward classes.

The decision of the government to implement the Mandal Commission Report was further challenged in the Apex Court as unconstitutional. A five judge bench of Supreme Court declared that "till it decides the constitutionality on the August 13, 1990, Notification of the National Front Government, no jobs will be given to the socially and educationally backward classes under the notification." The notification reserves 27 per cent job in the Central Civil Services and public sector undertakings on the basis of the Mandal Commission Report. In the judgment by the Supreme Court in the Mandal case on 10 November, 1992, it was upheld that two memoranda with the important qualifications that (a) the "creamy layer" or the backward classes should be excluded, because otherwise they would lap up all the benefits of reservations meant, (b) within four months the government should" specify the basis of exclusion, "whether on the basis of income, extent of holding or otherwise of the creamy layer, (c) the inclusion or exclusion of a caste or a section of a caste would have to be periodically reviewed to take care of changing circumstances, (d) permanent commissions should be appointed within four months by the Central Government and the State governments to decide regularly the cases which would arise involving questions whether a particular caste or a section of a caste was rightly included or excluded; and all further proceedings in such matters can be taken only in the Supreme Court, (e) "a backward caste" cannot be determined only and exclusively with reference to economic criterion, and therefore the 10 per cent additional reservations made by the second memorandum of 25 September, 1991, was illegal and void (f) armed forces and some higher civilian posts to be selected by the government should be outside the purview of caste reservations (g) reservations cannot be applied to promotion, "crutches cannot be provided throughout one's career."

In these judgments, the Supreme Court partially uphold the memoranda but subject to qualifications and conditions and secondly, declares that these memoranda providing for reservations on the caste basis are unconstitutional and void. In 1992, a nine judge Bench in the Indra Sawhney's case (popularly known as the Mandal Commission case) upheld 27 per cent quota for OBCs in Government jobs, subject to exclusion of 'creamy layers'. The Government soon identified the 'creamy layers' and recommendations of the Mandal Commission came into force at Centre and the states.

Since the implementation of Mandal report recommendations in 1990 for government jobs, the number of backward communities have grown due to continuous incorporation by various state governments. As of 2006, 2297 communities are listed as backward, an increase of more than 90 per cent from 1991, and no community has ever been removed from the list despite the progress made. Instead of coming up with more innovative ideas like making better provisions for primary education, checking dropouts from school, providing scholarships especially at higher levels, etc., the government has continued with a regressive reservation policy based on caste even after 58 years of independence.

Mandal II—On April 5, 2006, the declaration of the HRD Minister Arjun Singh to reserve 27 per cent of seats for OBCs in educational institutions funded by the central government like central universities, IITs, IIMs, AIIMS, and other professional institutions shook the whole nation. This reservation policy for the OBCs in educational institutions has been popularly referred to as Mandal II in the media. The 93rd Constitutional Amendment Act brought by the UPA government to supersede the Supreme Court judgment in the Inamdar case, that gave immunity to private educational institutions from reservation policy, was quoted as a constitutional mandate to extend the reservation policy in educational institutions. Arjun Singh's ambitious bid to introduce reservations for OBCs in Central Universities and autonomous institutions such as IIT, IIM and AIIMS relates to the unfinished business of the Mandal agenda. Though the Mandal Commission had recommended reservations for OBCs in jobs as well as educational institutions, the V.P. Singh Government came up with only job quota in August 1990. Arjun Singh's move to extend OBC quota to colleges run by Central government is a follow up that is coming sixteen years later in the vastly changed post liberalization scenario.

If implemented a large number of seats would go out of the general quota. According to a report by the *Times of India* seats in Delhi University alone would shrink by 13,716 seats-down from 35,306 seats to 21,590 seats. Fear of such far reaching consequences led to sharp reactions from the student communities in the institutes concerned, especially medical institutes. Doctors of AIIMS went on a strike with other doctors and students soon joining in. There have been nationwide protests as all the 20 central universities which are funded by the government were affected. Students from all over India soon gathered under the banner of "Youth for Equality" and demanded the government to roll back its decision to grant more reservations. Hunger strikes, candle light processions followed. The government and the police took stern measures to suppress the agitation. In Mumbai, on May 17, the police beat the peaceful anti-reservation agitators who were mainly medical students of King Edward and other medical colleges of Mumbai. Such excesses on the part of the police further added fuel to the fire. As anti-reservation agitation gathered pace, the Arjun Singh and UPA Government stayed adamant. However, when the protestors refused to bow down the government tried to douse the anti-reservation fire by hiking the number of seats in higher education so that the general category students do not lose out in any way. The government would then implement reservation upto 49.5 per cent from 2007. However, it was estimated that it would cost the national exchequer more than Rs. 8,000 crores and was feared by the students to be yet another empty promise on the part of the government and students refused to calm down.

In view of the entire confusion created by Mandal II, the "Supreme Court has asked the government to clarify two things: One, what is the basis for determining who belongs to the OBC category; and two, the rationale behind 27 per cent reservation for OBCs. It is again a time for appointing committees and dirty politics. The quota genie has been let out by the opportunist politicians once again and in the entire drama it is the students who stand to lose all."

MOILY COMMITTEE REPORT

An Oversight Committee was set up to prepare a comprehensive road map to implement 27 per cent reservations for the OBCs in the Central educational institutions. The Committee consisted of 13 members and was headed by former Karnataka Chief Minister, Veerappa Moily, to look into the issue of implementation of 27 per cent reservations for OBCs in higher educational institutions and requirements for increasing seats without reducing number in the general category.

Along with this, approved by the Prime Minister Manmohan Singh, the Oversight Committee with secretaries from the ministeries of HRD, Health and Family Welfare, Agriculture and Finance, were asked to submit its report by August.

The Oversight Committee headed by Veerappa Moily decided that reservations should be implemented in one go in all the centrally funded institutions, including the IITs and IIMs from 2007-08. A member of the Planning Commission said, "There is no question of staggering the implementation of reservations. The clear cut mandate of the oversight committee is to implement 27 per cent reservation for intake of the institutes of higher learning from the academic year 2007-08." Regarding the state funded, private and deemed universities, there is a proposal to implement reservations in a phased manner.

The major concern areas were not only to spruce up infrastructure to accommodate the extended OBC quotas a but also a 54 per cent enhancement of seats in Central educational institutions before the admission for the 2007-08 academic year.

The institutions required to upgrade infrastructure like classrooms laboratories and recruitment of teachers, all of which was not possible in one go. The Times of India mentions, "Rolling out quotas in less than a year would mean express recruitment, special procedures to cut down time for sanctions, quick tendering for new construction, hiring of premises to enhance learning space and faster disbursement of financial grants."

For working out a road map five sub-groups were formed to evaluate the needs of various universities and institutions to prepare themselves for quotas to be implemented within a year. The main agenda for the government was also to estimate financial and other resources needed to implement quotas.

As far as the expansion of infrastructure was concerned there were various bottlenecks which could be seen from that "expansion experience of the Indian Institute of Management, Ahmedabad." On June 28, 2006, Indian Express mentioned, "It took 20 years to get land, two years to plan and five years to implement its most recent expansion plan. The institute shared this experience with the oversight committee's sub-groups on management institutions at meetings in Bangalore and Chennai. . . . And the five year expansion plan 2002 (started) witnessing doubling of students by 2007. The roll out of the programmes has been a gradual process, where specific faculty members were selected, hostels were build and a new campus was planned over a period of time".

Moily infact, suggested rethinking the use of the term "reservations," which seems to be loaded with "negative connotation" and says, "The modern generation is resistant to reservation . . . in the US ..., Western Countries, it is called equal opportunities, affirmative action, diversity, plural society, ... time has come to change (our lexicon) from reservations."

A few key reforms incorporated by the oversight committee which is working on the roadmap to implement the 27 per cent OBC quota in Central Institutions was increasing faculty salaries beyond the limits imposed by the Pay Commission, in order to attract talent, pushing for more public-private partnership in the education sector, ensuring almost three fold increase in higher educational enrolment and reinforcing "global" brand equity of institutions of excellence.

The reason for introducing these changes and incorporating innovative ideas was the nation-wide protests against quota as Moily said was a "real conflict situation a policy decision resisted by people. Another reason was not only to fill the pot holes ... but to build a knowledge superhighway," and "to liberate India from ignorance."

Veerappa Moily, Head of the Oversight Committee said, "If we can liberalize the processes by which estimate are made and sanctions are granted, then the big leap is possible. We can treat the current situation as an opportunity to boost the per cent of the university-going people much beyond the current 8 per cent".

The Committee while ensuring that the number of general category seats is not reduced, point to the new quotas being introduced in one sweep. Moreover, the government is in favour of the new quotas being introduced in one sweep. For this the major concern areas was not only to spruce up infrastructure to accommodate the extended OBC quotas and 54 per cent enhancement in seats in central educational institutions, before the admission for the 2007-08 academic year. The institutes require to upgrade infrastructure like classroom, laboratories and recruit teachers, all of which cannot be possible in one go. S. Narayana, Dean of Academic Research at IIT Madras voicing a problem said, 'We need to go aggressive on faculty recruitment but the real problem is that there are not too many qualified people available'.

For working out a roadmap five sub-groups were formed to evaluate the needs of various universities and institutions to prepare themselves for quotas to be implemented within an year. The main agenda is also to estimate financial and other resources needed to implement quotas.

The Ministeries like Minority Affairs, Social Justice, Finance and Agriculture had sent their option to the HRD giving overwhelming support to the draft bill.

Yet, if the target of quantum job in seats is to be achieved in one years time, the faculty requirement had to go up and faculty recruitments was also a major problem to contend for there is lack of qualified people. The institutes would have to think of options and measures like recall retired faculty, demand to raise the retirement age, recruit people from other institutes in India, recruit people from abroad and so on. Enhancing infrastructure physical space, faculty intake, upgrading labs and laboratory equipments, more teachers, more classrooms, electricity, computers also was an immediate concern.

For this purpose, P. Chidambaram, Finance Minister had set aside Rs. 26.98 billion in the Budget 2007-08 for Central Educational Institutions under the Human Resource Development Ministry. A substantial amount was set aside for increasing the number of seats without dwindling with the general category seats, as suggested by the Oversight Committee. In the Budget 2008-09, approximately Rs. 25 billion have been allotted for Central Universities and higher educational institutions like IITs and IIMs.

However, a more rational alternative could have been to spend the resources not for the benefit of handful of OBC students, but spent in the fields of primary education and empowerment of the needy people irrespective of their caste. The current expansion of quotas has possibility of affecting the meritorious and the quality of education provided at the top institutions of the country, which should be taken care.

The Supreme Court in *Ashoka Kumar Thapur* vs. *Union of India* also known as Mandal II case, the Supreme Court's Constitution Bench paved the way for social justice in higher education and made an effort to answer about 25 raging questions on India's pursuit of affirmative action in higher educational institutions. The judgment "marked the achievement of a milestone in the struggle of the backward classes in the country for a greater share in educational opportunities than what they had been entitled to until then."

The Bench in its hearing was making an attempt to dispose of certain public interest petitions which were filed to challenge the constitutionality of the 93rd Constitution Amendment Act, which added Article 15(5) of the Constitution, which enabled the state to make any special provision for the SCs, STs and other backward tribes for their admission to educational institutions, including private educational institutions, whether aided or unaided by the state, except minority educational institutions. The validity of the Central Educational Institutions (Reservation in Admission) Act, 2006, which makes special provisions for the candidates belonging to the SCs, STs and OBCs was challenged by the petitioners. The Chief Justice K.G. Balakrishnan in the main judgment delivered said:

"The 93rd Constitution Amendment Act, inserting Article 15(5), does not violate the basic structure so far as it relates to aided educational institutions." He added, "The Central Educational Institutions (Reservation in Admission) Act, 2006, is constitutionally valid, subject to the exclusion of creamy layer . . . the quantum of 27 per cent reservation for OBCs is not illegal . . . The 2006 Act is not illegal merely because a time limit is not prescribed for reservation . . . There should be a review of the lists of socially and educationally backward classes (SEBCs) every five years."

So the validity of the 93rd Amendment and the 2006 Act was upheld by the Bench almost unanimously in the discussions which began on August 7, 2007 and ended in November 1, 2007.The Supreme Court rejected the government's reasons for non-exclusion of creamy layer from the OBCs and unanimously directed the government to issue a notification excluding the creamy layer from the Act's OBC beneficiaries.

The Supreme Court, a little later, "saw through the Centre's attempts to build a backlog of upfilled 27 per cent OBC quota seats in central educational institutions and said not releasing vacant seats to the general category would be counter-productive." The Bench comprising of Chief Justice K.G. Balakrishnan and Justice Arijit Pasayat, C.K. Thakkar, R.V. Raveendran and Dalveer Bhandari, which had recommended "the quota with creamy layer exclusion" also believed that keeping seats vacant would be counter productive and said "the judgment was crystal clear about allowing vacant quota seats to be filled by the general category."

CHAPTER 7

Reservations: A Myth or Reality

THE QUAGMIRE OF CASTE RESERVATION

The unique stratification in the form of the caste system is present in the Indian society, whose rigidity makes social mobility a cumbersome process. Dr. Ambedkar had rightly observed that just as leapord cannot change its spots, a Hindu cannot change his caste. "People at the lowest rung of the caste system, are still facing the harsh reality of untouchability. The only way out seems to be through legal protection, entailing a legal process which has to be caste based. So, the reservations become imperative in our society where caste based prejudices exist."

The concept of caste-based reservations for government jobs and seats in institutions have been around ever since India gained independence in 1947. The Mandal Commission—whose report forms the basis of the current proposal- identified 3,743 castes and sub-castes as OBC in its report in 1980. Needless to say, there in an argument that such crude categorization is both unjust and arbitrary. But vote-bank politics has always prevented a serious questioning of the entire push towards reservations.

During the last forty five years the reservation have continued to exist and have become higher with passing years. The government, due to its vested interests, continue to reserve more and more seats and expanded the periphery of reservations to the SCs, the STs and the OBCs. Under the guise of reservation the government has taken care of its vested interests.

Besides the 27 per cent proposed reservation for the OBCs, there is already a 22.5 per cent reservations for the Scheduled Castes and Schedule Tribes (SC\ST) groups in these educational institutions. Mr. Singh's proposals raised the reservation percentage for SCs, STs and OBCs up to 49 per cent. This applied to all premier institutions in India, including the universities. Mr. Singh with an aim to go further, last December tabled the 104th amendment to the Constitution to ensure that reservations were also extended to private unaided educational institutions. Job quotas in the private sector, it is often said, 'is only a matter of time' although shelved for the present time.

Predictably, the reaction of the industry has been hostile. Azim Premji—CEO of Wipro spoke publicly against the proposal. He is one among many entrepreneurs who have expressed their dissatisfaction over the proposals. However, industrial bodies such as the Confederation of Indian Industries (CII) are already preparing themselves for the consequences. A "caste head count" has been launched among the national workforce of these companies in order to gauge how the various castes are represented. The theoretical arguments around this issue are complex, and academic debates surrounding the American system of affirmative action the reverse discrimination have been around since the 1970s. Much of that debate applies to the situation currently prevalent in India.

The opponents of reservations put forward various arguments against the issue. The first major argument in favour of the reservations is that of historic injustice being dished out to the subaltern classes. However, the notion of inter-generational guilt is somewhat disturbing to our democratic institutions and raises a query. Why should someone suffer today because his ancestors might have wronged another individual? Therefore, the opponents argue that allocating quotas on the basis of caste is a form of social discrimination which is contrary to the right to equality. As a consequence, legislation for providing reservation for Christian and Muslim religious minorities in all government education institutions will be introduced, which is contrary to the idea of secularism, and is a form of discrimination on the basis of religion.

Reservation policy in India has not helped to ameliorate the conditions of 'most disadvantaged' amongst the backward section. "The creamy layer" i.e. Beneficiaries amongst the members of the minority groups who are well off, attempt to monopolize the opportunities. The reservations are, infact, benefiting not the impoverished among the needy and downtrodden members of OBC and other reserved category, but redistributing the benefits to the better off amongst them, thus, making the aim of reservation total failure. Moreover, the children of those who have benefited from reservations continue to take advantage of quotas. Political parties know reservations are no way to improve the lot of the poor and the backward. They support them because of self-interest of the "creamy layer," who use the reservations to further their own family interests, and as a political flag of 'achievement' during election campaigns. In fact, several studies show that the OBC class is quite comparable with the general caste in terms of annual per capita consumption expenditure, and the top strata of OBC is ahead in most of the consumption areas. The layer can be excluded from the orbit of reservations for not everyone from the so-called upper class are rich and not all from so-called lower classes are poor.

Moreover, the candidates from the so-called creamy layer could find ways of fudging income proofs to avail themselves of the OBC quota. Udit Raj, National President of the Indian Justice Party as well as president of the All India Confederation of SC/ST Organisations, told the Frontline (*Frontline* May 9, 2008), "It is like the NREGS (National Rural Employment

Guarantee Scheme) or the targeted system of public distribution. Most of the NREGS beneficiaries and the BPL (below poverty line) card holders are not those who are poor others have benefited it their cost."

By making caste a criterion for social benefits derived from reservations, the government is, infact, perpetuating the caste system. More and more groups have come under the umbrella of OBC and reservations have expanded a lot. It has became more extensive and applies to many fields including government contracting, higher education and legislative office.

The backward groups are becoming more and more conscious about their position, often leading to adverse relationship between the members of the reserved categories and general categories of the society. Casteism has always been a subject of controversy in our country. Caste distinctions divide the society and overall development of individuals and the growth of the country will suffer.

The reservation policies have conflicting consideration with the considerations of merit and it is quite likely that less qualified candidates are selected at the cost of more qualified candidates. Example, in a sharp critique of the Mandal recommendations, Ashok Guha has written that 'reservations in public employment impair the efficiency and quality of public service by reducing the average competence standards of civil service entrants, reducing their incentive to perform well and their motivation to improve, undermine the moral of workers and supervisors and stimulate caste conflict in public institutions, thus harming team work and co-operation. In the field of higher education, most quota students might not be able to meet the standards of IITs, IIMs and other Indian Institutes which are globally acknowledged'.

The educational institutions such as the IITs and IIMs have been at the forefront of the changing face of India under globalization. They produce much of the skilled workforce for the top Indian and multinational corporations. Merit—rather than caste or religious background-should be the sole criteria of selection in such institutions, so as not to promote mediocrity which will hamper the quality of these institutions.

The most popular and plausible argument against reservation is that meritorious students suffer because of reservation. The general category students are feeling deprived, for reserved seats are taking away their chances of success. The deserving and bright students might be compelled to go abroad for higher education and employment, because of the reservation policy. So, when it is also argued that reservations ensure a route to upward social mobility for the downtrodden and it gives them self-respect and dignity as citizens, it is extremely doubtful how far the dignity of the individual is being preserved by leapfrogging him into a position for which a better qualified candidate already exists. It helps to breed a mentality that people from backward castes can only get a job with the help of quotas, and it is humiliating to well-qualified candidates from such communities so, it works adversely for both the sides, the members of lower classes still feel they do not have sufficient representation and the members of upper classes feel that inspite of their merits, they do not have same opportunities. Even for the reserved category it is working otherwise. Anand Kumar in this regard, comments, "Today because of these relaxations, these candidates are not considered up to the mark." They are branded as non-meritorious, incapable, inefficient and so on. Gautam Kumar, an OBC and ex-IITian said that "growing up in Bihar, he was always made to feel responsible for his caste. When he made to IIT, Kharag pur, as a general candidate he finally threw away that tag. But now, with the education quota for OBCs, he feels 'targeted' again." In wake of OBC reservations at IITs, IIMs etc. he urged the leaders of the nation not to bring separation on the basis of birth, for it will endanger the unity of our nation and said, "Please let the new generation of India live in a world where ideas matter, not the caste or religion into which one is born."

The future of the entire country is said to be in danger because of the reservations. Indeed, the Supreme Court had recently questioned the states for not collecting data on individuals from SC, ST and OBC backgrounds who serve jobs and secure educational seats through the 'general' category than their respective caste categories.

Then, the anti-reservation argument runs as such that there are so many efforts already made to give proper primary education to really deprived classes, so there is no need to reserve seats for higher studies. The government schools in India have absolutely no comparison to the public schools in the developed countries, and only about 65 per cent of the Indian population is literate, the functional literacy being estimated to be even as low as only 34 per cent of the population. The critics argue that "reservation" only in higher institutions and jobs, without improving primary and secondary education, moreover, cannot solve this problem. The government is dividing the people on the basis of castes for the political advantages they can avail. This can even lead to prolonged reservation system, for an indefinite period of time, as the government has been increasing the scope and ambit of reservations. The caste system is kept alive through these measures. Instead of coming up with alternative innovative ideas which ensures equal representation and at the same time making the caste system irrelevant, the decision will further perpetuate the caste system. This would increase the caste hatred in the country leading to aggravated tensions in the institutions of the higher education.

The autonomy of the higher educational institutions and 'deemed universities' are lost due to reservations and control of government is established over it. Arjun Singh's proposed Bill i.e. The Central Education Institutions (Reservation of Seats and Regulation of Admission and Fee) that seeks to give the Central government power to regulate the fees of all deemed universities as well as their selection procedure, also introduces a differential fee structure for SC, ST and OBC and the general category students and this will ultimately be at the cost of general category students. Moreover, the Centre will have say in the amount which is to be fixed.

The government might be pursuing for 27.5 per cent reservations for OBCs, but the fact remains that even the 22.5 per cent SC and ST quota in higher educational institutions remains unfilled. The data collected by HRD Ministry for 2003-04 show that out of the total number of students in higher educational institution *i.e.* a little over one crore, only 16 per cent are SCs and STs. This clearly indicates that out of the existing quota, 6.5 per cent of reserved seats are going vacant. Even after providing so many facilities to reserved categories during education, if there is no adequate representation of these sections in the work force, the problem must be with the education system. Admission on the basis of caste will only act as a discouraging factor and a sense of inferiority will prevail among the students belonging to the lower castes.

Moreover, even the 27 percent OBC quota which has been there since almost twelve years has almost never been filled. "In the 2005 batch of recruitments, announced in May 2006, the proportion was down at an all-time low of 20.2 percent. Only once in the last 12 batches—the 1997 batch—has it come close to matching the stipulated 27 percent, when it was 26.7 percent."

The increasing reservations will lead to proliferation in the lists enumerating OBC. There has already been a 90 per cent increase in the number of centrally notified OBCs, *i.e.* from 1,257 castes in 1993 to 2,297 in 2006.

In the opinion of India Inc., reservation would dilute the quality of corporate activity. Moreover, if reservations are extended to the private sector than Multinational companies will be deterred by this action of the government, and foreign investment in India may reduce, hurting the growth of the Indian economy. Doubtless, urgent action to improve the lot of the majority, which has not benefited from development—not achieved after years of reservations for Scheduled Castes—is essential. But this must not adversely affect the improvement of the economy's competitiveness in a very competitive world.

So, it is argued that must look at 'genesis of merit' rather than take it at face value. The argument is that the backward castes never got adequate access to public services such as education, health, etc. to develop their intellect and compete in a truly meritocratic society. This appears intuitively attractive, but it leaves a big question unanswered.

After all, there are poor people in India who are from the 'general' caste category. On the contrary, there are well-off people from the backward castes. These might be the exception to the norm, but their existence cannot be denied. By implementing caste-based reservations, all we achieve is to discriminate against the poor-but-upper caste candidate and benefit the "creamy layer" amongst the rich-but-lower caste candidate. It has been suggested that reservations should be should be made on the economic class of the candidate—a criteria that cuts across caste boundaries when making a decision. However, even this system is not adequate. Given India's high rate of corruption and poor administrative setup, 'faking poverty' could indeed be rife. In any case this also compromises meritocracy.

The concept of reservations can be used as a constructive tool of social engineering and building a society based on social justice. It would be injustice to treat two unequals equally as much as to treat two equals unequally. In a highly in egalitarian Indian society, protective policies are unavoidable for inclusive development. The pro-reservations arguments can be enumerated as below:

- If reservations are not encouraged then the number of the members of backward communities who are considering higher education will reduce. These candidates would not even consider higher education or apply for admission to selective higher education institutions without the reservations.
- Reservations helps in representing the diverse population of the country, even the backward ones into the universities. This diverse student body enables universities to provide a better educational experience for all students, which eventually enhance their ability to function in a multi-cultural society like

India. The multi-cultural interaction at the level of University, enables the students to learn how to function better as workers and citizens in a multi-cultural society. Such a cultural understanding will enhance people's ability to play a constructive role as citizens in a democracy.

- Reservations are measure to provide legal protection against caste prejudices. It facilities representation and assimilation of the backward sections into the mainstream. Due to historical oppression it is not fair to expect the oppressed classes to compete with so-called upper class students. These measure can somehow help to undo centuries of oppression. Reservations are a measure to counter the tilt in favour of the upper caste.
- The reservations have been present in states like Tamil Nadu for many years and have produced good results in promoting social justice without compromising quality. In wake of 2006 protests by the anti-reservationist it was said that it was almost wholly a north-Indian phenomena with no resonance in the southern states." It is mainly due to the people's movement during the early 20th century and reservations have been introduced there as early as 1920. As a result, a multitude of professionals belong to the backward communities in the southern states even in the best medical institutions.
- According to M. Anandakrishnan, former Vice-Chancellor of Anna University and Southern Regional Head of the All India Council for Technical Education, 'there is no evidence whatsoever that the quality of education in premier institutions has deteriorated because of admitting students from the disadvantaged sections of society on the basis of the reservation policy.' His argument is that for every ten students admitted under the reservation policy there are at least 1,000 to 2,000 competitors in that

category which means that those who get selected from the reserved classes are the best from the lot. And Anandakrishnan adds: 'In fact, the motivation factor among people coming from the reservation category is higher because they are mostly from the first generation of learners and are looking for upward social and economic mobility.' Another argument is that there is a difference between the concept of reservations and the relaxations attached with it. The minor relaxation (if 5 percent) makes people question about the merit of SCs or STs. Anand Kumar suggests, "Considering the development of the last 50 years these relaxations can be phased out beginning with the creamy layer. But reservations have to continue to provide legal protection in the face of the 'no entry' syndrome against the Dalits."

- In case of admissions to engineering, medicine and other professional courses are concerned, at the entry level, there is hardly any difference between the marks obtained by the general category and OBC students and the SC, ST and OBC students have to undertake the same examination and tests.

  The Supreme Court in *Post Graduate Institute of Medical Education and Research* vs. *K.L. Narsimhan* asserts that "the benefit of reservation, does not necessarily imply down-grading the excellence, and the student who is inducted through reservations "is also expected to have the same degree of excellence." It declares, "As stated earlier the benefit of reservation does not necessarily imply down-grading the excellence. Every student after admission into the post-graduate specialty or super-specialty is required to undergo the same course of study, same standard and higher performance for qualifying the courses for conferment of the degrees in the respective specialties or super-specialty or technical subjects. In that regard, there is no relaxation given to the candidates belonging to reserved categories."

- The whole issue of reservation is not against Article 15 (Right to Equality) of the Constitution because Article 15(4) says that the government can take necessary steps for the upliftment of socially and educationally backward classes. Although, Arun Shourie emphasises on the fact that "injustices are exaggerated to legitimize what the politician has, for other reasons, found convenient." He warns to "be alert to the way catch expressions—'the poor', 'the backwards', 'social justice'—are being used to undermine standards, to flout norms, to put institution to work—not for the millions in those categories but for the ones who have fooled those millions with those catch phrases."

The following policy changes have been suggested to counter the hike in quotas and to find a solution to the problem.

- The unavailability of seats is not as big a problem to the SC, ST and OBC as their financial crunch is and assistance may be provided in the forms of scholarships.
- The expenditure on higher and technical education is 0.4 per cent and 0.1 per cent of GDP respectively, which should be raised.
- The number of seats in premier institutes should be increased, but then the quality of education should not be hampered, to attain which, it will be necessary to increase the teaching faculty as well along with the infrastructure.
- People who are tax payers or children of tax payers should not be eligible for reservation. This will ensure that benefits will reach the poorest of the poor and India will achieve social justice.
- Progeny of those who have got a position through

quota should be denied the same privilege. One 'quota-case' in every family is sufficient.

- Reservations in premier institutes are of no use unless creamy layer of students is kept out of it.
- The misuse of the quota by the powerful and the rich should be taken care of. Proper investigations and checks must be undertaken by the ministers who so loudly advocate the reservation regime.
- The level of primary and secondary education must be boosted. All the problems are from primary level itself, if a student does not have a strong base, then he cannot complete higher education successfully. The government should make efforts to uplift backward classes by strengthening the educational base of these classes at the primary level. Caste does not define how intelligent a person is.

  The government should focus upon universal school education in all areas especially in areas dominated by SC, ST and OBC. Good school facilities should be provided to the special incentives like free tution fees, school books, mid-day meals etc. Financial aid and assistance should be provided to needy students from weaker sections.
- Increase the number of higher education institutes. For example, only a handful of good engineering institutes for a country of one thousand million, aspiring to become an economic and political power in the world is not sufficient at all. So, the focus should be on improving infrastructure.
- Once a person gets a job on the basis of the quotas it should not be extended to his/her children as it would make the community complacent and also at the same time deny opportunities to other more deserving candidates from the lower community. Essentially a shrinking population base that needs upliftment will happen by adopting this policy.

- Current reservation proposals only seem attractive to people who support it but it is of no use to millions of people who are leading a very pathetic life in India due to condition of object poverty irrespective of caste. Right approach would be to provide them with proper primary education, to prevent their drop out from schools and making them "natural competitors" and to give scholarships at the higher levels rather than forcing 50 per cent reservation. A recent example of this approach is when backward class and village students from one of the most under-developed states Bihar made it to IIT in the general category, all due to proper guidance and economic help. However, the initiative was from private sector, not government effort.
- Another alternative is to provide equal access and equal opportunity to free education to everyone, irrespective of caste, creed and economic status, right from the primary level. Special incentives should be permitted to weaker sections. A time bound programme had been proposed by Bhangara of the National Knowledge Commission, with more emphasis on primary education and excluding the creamy layer from reservations.

The solution that we propose is two-tier. *Firstly*, we must identify the crux of the problem-continuing caste discrimination. The government should focus on implementing the laws for equal opportunity and access to public services in the remote villages in India's heartlands. Second, the selection criteria for institutions must be based on a subjective criterion which take into account economic condition of the applicant's family, his merit and the implications of his/her particular caste background, etc.

Caste, therefore, must be *one* of the factors under consideration, and only in so far as it actually did have an impact on the concerned individual's life. Such a tailor-made criterion will look at every person individually and will not blindly follow a rule that may not be neutral or fair at all. It discourages precedence-based judgments being made.

Therefore, there will be no need for quotas in any state-based institutions whatsoever. As far as private sector reservations is concerned, the rights of the individuals who invested their private assets to build a company will be grossly infringed upon, were they forced to hire someone based on the caste's criterion and not their own choice. It is, therefore, a classical oxymoron.

There is a consequentialist argument for caste-based quota. It argues that we must wait for a generation to operate under the system for results to be evident. However, that misses the entire point. The counter-argument is not that quotas will not work, but that it is inherently unjust.

Reservations in jobs or higher education is a measure of solving the problem of disadvantaged at the higher end which has to be supplemented by measures to improve the quality of teaching at primary level and teaching at the government school so, we need to ensure teaching especially in the rural areas. By investing in human capital, India can succeed in the globalised world.

The reservation policy might not solve the basic problems facing the country but it will certainly help in bringing the ST, SC and OBC community into the mainstream of the society. It is all the more essential to do this because of discrimination faced by it and we cannot expect any miracle to happen in a short span of almost 60 years of reservations and other measures. If the SC, ST and OBC constituting a large chunk of our population, are left behind in terms of economic and social advancement, it is a disgrace for all of us who have done nothing to remedy it.

Our basic aim is to achieve a more egalitarian society that is committed to standards of excellence in every field. The supporters of the reservation argue that these underprivileged castes has been deprived of equal opportunity for good education. Reservation has been used as a measure to abridge the gap between prosperous upper castes and the backward sections. Our basic objective is to secure justice for everyone not necessarily for the people belonging to SCs, STs and OBCs. We have to strive create an egalitarian social order guaranteeing equal opportunities to all and fight against all sources of inequality, exclusion and discrimination.

CHAPTER 8

Reservation for the SCs and STs

An indelible feature of the Indian political scene has been emergence of the SCs and STs as an entity. Dalits, for long have been denied the rights to fulfill their human aspirations. For centuries, the Scheduled Castes and the Scheduled Tribes have suffered intense social and economic discrimination because of the caste system. According to Manu Smriti, the position of Brahmins was superior for they have been created by God and hold the prerogative to be learned, to be rich, to be kings, to be noble and also, above all laws. A majority of the population, as a result of the dominance of the ruling castes over then, lost their separate identity and were considered out castes.' They were forced to live in total isolation from the rest of society. There was no possibility of upward mobility for them. They were assigned to take up the most menial labour and faced a lot of hardships. These communities were called as the depressed classes. It is said that "the disease of untouchability is fairly old in our society. It generated social hatred and discriminating feeling of high and low, and as a result the later category suffered for centuries in the hands of the former."

The grounds of the political emergence of the SCs can be traced from the end of the nineteenth century and the beginning of the twentieth century, when single organization of the depressed Classes from different parts of the British India came forward with their demands. It was also largely influenced by the various attempts made by the British, including the Government of India Act, 1935, which incorporated the reservation of the seats for the depressed classes. This Act introduced the term "Scheduled Castes" for the first time. Infact, Ambedkar even pioneered the reservation policy as early as the 1920s, mainly on the basis of widespread and ubiquitous discriminatory and exclusionary character of Hindu society towards the former untouchables. In the year 1942, Ambedkar established the All India Depressed Classes Federation to support the advancement of the Scheduled Castes. He also raised the issue of reservations for the Scheduled Castes in government services and education. After independence, Ambedkar was appointed as the Chairman of the Drafting Committee for the Indian Constitution.

Since the Scheduled Castes are said to suffer from social segregation, and the Scheduled Tribes from geographic isolation, the Constitutional provisions and legislative reservations, were intended to uplift these populations and guarantee their representation in government.

In view of this position, the framers of the Indian Constitution incorporated in the Constitution the provisions for affirmative action or compensatory discrimination as termed by few. As Andre Beteille mention that the SCs and STs share the common disabling feature of "exteriority," although the nature of exteriority from which they suffer differ in origin and its practice, as well. The SCs have suffered from "segregation" and the STs from geographical "isolation." The measures of protective discrimination of affirmative action for the SCs arose since they have been victims of the practice of untouchability and also other forms of discrimination and grave social injustices. So, the upliftment was ensured through introducing reservations of jobs for dalits in the government, employment and reservations of seats for them in educational institutions.

The founding fathers of the Constitution introduced the reservation policy for backward classes identified as the Scheduled Castes (SCs) and the Scheduled Tribes (STs) for only ten years initially. They knew that the reservation policy has an impact on the Fundamental Right to Equality. Another factor which they were aware of was that this policy of reservations would strengthen the feeling of caste and tribe segregation as well.

THE SCHEDULED CASTES AND THE SCHEDULED TRIBES

The term Scheduled Caste is identified with erstwhile untouchable or the exterior castes who had been subjected to various offences, humiliation and harassment and atrocities of all forms. They were segregated and not allowed access to many civic amenities. The access to education was denied to them and could not make a standing of their own in economic and social life. According to 1981 census together, they constitute 23.5 per cent of the total population of the country, the Scheduled Castes 15.8 per cent and Scheduled Tribes 7.7 per cent. There is however, state-wise variation in the proportion of the Scheduled Castes and the Scheduled Tribes population. The Scheduled Castes are concentrated in Punjab, Uttar Pradesh, Himachal Pradesh, West Bengal and Haryana, the Scheduled Tribes are concentrated in the North eastern states, Union Territories of Arunachal Pradesh and Mizoram, in Gujarat, Madhya Pradesh, Maharashtra, Orissa and Rajasthan and in certain other Union Territories;. Dadra and Nagar Haveli, Lakshadweep, Andaman and Nicobar Islands. The term was first coined by the Simon Commission and embodied in the Government of India Act, 1935. In 1936, British government published a list of Scheduled Castes, "The so-called Schedule is a list of castes enlisted to parliamentary seats, public employment and special educational benefits. Thus, the scheduling or placing under a list was taken into account for providing certain protection and framing schemes in the matter of reservations in service on community basis. Thus, the term Scheduled Caste is a British invention."

So, "the term Scheduled Castes comes in the line of categories like Out castes, Depressed castes and Extension Castes created by the British administrators. While the term has useful moral neutrality, it is essentially legal in nature: the people in question have been transformed into a special legal class of citizens for certain purpose of the State."

According to Article 341 of the Constitution of India, "The President may with respect to any State or Union Territory, after Consultation with the Governor thereof, by public notification, specify the castes, races or tribes, which shall for the purpose of this Constitution be deemed to be Scheduled Castes in relation to that State or Union Territory, as the case may be."

Moreover, "Parliament may by a law include in or exclude from the list of Scheduled Castes specified in a notification issued under the Clause, i) any caste, race or tribe, or part of, or group, within any caste, race or tribe, but save as aforesaid, a notification issued under the said clause shall not be varied by any subsequent notification."

Winmick's Dictionary of Anthropology has defined tribe, "as a social group usually with a definite areas, dialect, cultural homogeneity and unifying social organization." The term Scheduled Tribes has been used for the first time in the Constitution of India and the earlier expression used in pre-independence days were aboriginal tribes, backward tribes etc. Tribal people have long been living in far-flung hilly and forest habitations, somewhat cut off from the mainstream of Indian society. They are people who through the ages have lived in abject material poverty and conditions of exclusion.

THE CONSTITUTIONAL PROVISIONS

The Constitution of the country, gave recognition to the Scheduled Castes and the Scheduled Tribes as the two most backward groups needing special protection.

The constitutional provisions intended to safeguard the interests of the SCs and STs are Article 17 mentioning abolition of untouchability and prohibition of its practice is any form and Article 23, mentioning prohibition of 'begar' or forced or bonded labour.

Under Article 15(A) special provisions may be made for the advancement of any socially and educationally backward class and for the Scheduled Castes and the Scheduled Tribes. The "advancement" meant here is again in any field. This sub-clause (4) of Article 15 was inserted by an amendment in 1951. Article 16(4) permits the state to make any provision for the reservation of appointments or posts in favour of any backward class, which, in the opinion of the state, is not adequately represented in the services under it. The expression "backward class" in this sub-clause is interpreted by the Supreme Court to mean "socially and educationally backward" as is specifically mentioned in the sub-clause (4) added later to Article 15.

The Constitution of India makes provision for the reservation of seats for the Scheduled Castes and Scheduled Tribes in the Parliament and in the State Legislatures (Article 330 and Article 332 respectively). It was initially mentioned in the Constitution of India, that the reservation would be only for a period of ten years. But, the Constitution has been amended from time to time with the extension of the period of 10 years. At present the position is that the reservations will cease after 60 years i.e. after 2010 (79th Amendment Act, 1999 in Article 334).

Article 335 of the Constitution provides that in making appointment in public employment, "the claims of the members of the Scheduled Castes and the Scheduled Tribes shall be taken into consideration, consistently with the maintenance of efficiency of administration." The 82nd Amendment Act, 2000, further provides for "relaxation in qualifying marks in any examination or lowering the standards of evaluation for reservation in matters of promotion for dalits."

Article 338 makes provision for the Constitution of a National Commission for the Scheduled Castes and Scheduled Tribes. Article 338(5)(6) makes it the duty of the Commission to enquire into specific complaints with respect to deprivation of rights ad safeguards of the dalits.

In the year 2000, 1294 complaints were received by the Commission for examining and further action. The Constitution also provides that the Union and State Governments should consult the Commission on all major policy matters affecting the Scheduled Castes and Scheduled Tribes.

Article 341 empowers the President to specify by a public notification the castes, races or tribes or parts of groups within castes, races or tribes as the Scheduled Castes for purposes of the Constitution. The notification with respect to as state should be made after consulting the governor of the state. Article 342 provides for a similar notification with respect to the Scheduled Tribes (1984:46).

Article 341 states: Scheduled Castes – (1) The President may with respect to any State or Union Territory, and where it is a State, after consultation with the Governor thereof, by public notification, specify the castes, races or tribes or part of or groups within castes, races or tribes which shall for the purpose of this Constitution be deemed to be Scheduled Castes in relation to that State or Union Territory as the case may be (Article 341, Constitution of India).

Article 342 states: Scheduled Tribes – (1) The President may with respect to any State or Union Territory, and where it is a State, after consultation with the Governor thereof, by public notification, specify the tribes or tribal communities or part of or groups within tribes or tribal communities which shall for the purpose of this Constitution be deemed to be Scheduled Tribes in relation to that State or Union Territory as the case may be (Article 342, the Constitution of India). The Indian Constitution is conspicuous in that it is the duty of the state to uplift the weaker sections of society like the Scheduled Castes and the Scheduled Tribes, has been built into the provisions of the Constitution, instead of leaving it to the administrative policies and their approval by the judiciary. The general spirit behind the concern of the Constitution for weaker sections reflected in the Directive Principles of the State Policy laid down in Article 46, which states:

> The State shall promote with special care the educational and economic interests of the weaker sections of the people, and in particular of the Scheduled Castes and the Scheduled Tribes and shall protect from them from social injustice and all forms of exploitation.

POSITIVE DISCRIMINATION MEASURES

The various positive discrimination measures are the distinctive features of the Constitution of India. The provision for "reservations" in favour of two disadvantaged groups, namely, the Scheduled Castes and the Scheduled Tribes are seen as the mainstay of Indian democracy. These reservations include three types of provisions, (i) reservations in the State Legislatures and the Union Legislature or Parliament, (ii) reservations in services and posts in government services, and (iii) reservations of seats in the educational institutions.

Dr. Ambedkar elucidated the vision to provide representation to the Scheduled Castes and Scheduled Tribes in the educational, professional and political institutions. He said, "There shall be no disabilities attaching to anyone on the ground of his being a member of the Depressed Classes in regard to any elections to local bodies or appointment to public services. Every endeavour shall be made to secure fair representation of the depressed classes in these respects, subject to such educational qualifications as may be laid down for appointment to public services."

Education is considered as a key to social mobility. It is also pre-requisite to avail the constitutional safeguards especially of employment and educational advancement. Andre Betleile comments, "Only with educational advancement, and educational advancement can come about only with socio-economic advancement, their educational condition can be a crucial indicator of their overall status as beneficiaries of the implementation of the various constitutional provisions, and consequently can lay claim for a role in decision-making process."

There has been a significant rise in education of the Scheduled Castes and the Scheduled Tribes as a result of educational programmes. Along with the provisions of reservations, the major programs that have been developed for the purpose include exemption from school fees, provisions for stipends or scholarships, provisions for facilities like book grants, and maintenance of hostels, or assistance to hostels for students from the Scheduled Castes and the Schedule Tribes.

The central government provides for and also sponsors the postmatric scholarships, for college education, award of travel grants and reservation in favour of Scheduled Castes in merit scholarships. The programmes also provide for assistance by way of special coaching for Scheduled Castes and Scheduled Tribe students residing in hostels and pre-examination coaching facilities for students appearing in competitive examinations.

In 1931, the literacy rate among the Scheduled Castes was 1.90 per cent as against the general literacy of 9.6 per cent. In 1971, the literacy rose to 14.71 per cent as against the general average of 29 per cent. Thus, the coefficient of equality rose from 25 per cent to 50 per cent. A noteworthy improvement in the field of education is the institution of the postmatric scholarship scheme, that is scholarships are granted to finance education after the high school stage. The number of Scheduled Caste students who utilized it in 1944 was 114, and it steadily increased to 390,000 in 1978-79, the number of Scheduled Tribes pupils availing the benefit in 1978-79 was 70,000.

However, the literacy gap between the Scheduled Castes and the Scheduled Tribes continues. As compared to All India literacy rates of 46.9 per cent and 24.8 per cent for males and females respectively, the literacy rates for the Scheduled Castes males and females stood at 31.1 per cent and 10.9 per cent respectively in 1981. The corresponding percentages for the Scheduled Tribes were still lower at 24.5 per cent and 8.0 per cent respectively. Even the enrolment of Scheduled Castes and Scheduled Tribes also registered substantial increase over the last three decades at all educational levels.

The National Policy in Education (NPE), 1986 aimed at universal enrollment of all Dalit children in 6-11 age group and 75 per cent enrollment in 11-14 age groups as well as the successful completion by them of primary and middle school stages by the year 1990. Although, the Report on the Programme of Action of National Educational Policy, 1986 mentioned that "enrolment by itself is of little importance if children do not continue education beyond even a year, many of them not seeing the school for more than a few days." The report also included the fact that nearly 60 per cent of the children drop out between classes I-V and 75 per cent between classes I-VIII and that nearly 22 per cent of the enrolled at the primary states are outside 6-11 age group, mostly over-aged. The corresponding percentages amongst the SCs is still higher because of evident reasons. At the further higher levels of education, their enrolment ratio shrinks and dropout rate enhances.

In the revised programme of action in 1992, these targets were reiterated. The District Primary Education Programme (DPEP), which is on the educational landscape of India since 1990s, emphasis is upon improved access, participation and achievement in children from the marginalized groups. The Sarva Shiksha Abhiyan introduced in the year 2000, stressed upon the involvement of dalit communities in the ownership of school committees, setting up of alternative schooling facilities in unreserved habitations, monitoring attendance and retention of Dalit children, using community teachers etc. All these measures aim for the betterment and well being of the Dalits, Tribals and the downtrodden.

The job reservations provisions are not mandatory, they are enabling provisions. The Constitution mentions that the state may take such measures as are necessary for the special benefit of the Other Backward Classes.

Another important objective was to secure an adequate representation of SCs and STs in the public service and for this provision of reservations has been made in the Constitution. Despite all these efforts, there is a lack of strong educational foundation in the students of reserved categories and poor educational system seems to be the major cause. According to the parliamentary committee report on the welfare for the Scheduled Castes and the Scheduled Tribes in Delhi University between 1995-2000, only 50 per cent of the seats reserved for the Scheduled Castes and 33 per cent of the seats reserved for the Scheduled Tribes were filled. Even for two each academic year, in IIT Delhi for the under graduate admissions, only nearly 67 per cent of the seats reserved for the Scheduled Castes and the Scheduled Tribes were filled.

Various other problems faced in implementing the policy of educational reservations are reluctance of prestigious educational institution, inability of students admitted under the policy of reservations to cope with academic requirements, uneven representation of different Scheduled Castes in education, increasing resentment against Scheduled Castes on the part of the non-Scheduled Castes, etc. Due to this provision the representation of the SCs in the Central Service has increased over the years, although this has been adequate only in class IV jobs and less in all the four classes of jobs. Moreover, the scheme was not implemented in the same spirit as mentioned in the constitution and there is a very wide gap between the policy and the actual position.

The policy of reservation helped some of the capable families among the Scheduled Castes and Scheduled Tribes. Many of them were successful in reaping the benefits of reservations and they entered the government jobs and climbed up the ladder of promotion by its help. Those who were ignorant, illiterate and extremely poor were unable to reap the benefit of reservation. There was hardly any improvement of the position of depressed classes.

The forward families amongst the SC or ST have availed the benefit of reservation to a large extent. "One can see that son of an IAS Officer on reservation becoming IAS or allied personnel on reservation. One can see in single family of SC or ST there are 51 IPS officers whereas another family of SC/ST is languishing in object poverty, beyond description. The position of families hitherto enjoying reservations was never reviewed.

The Constitution also makes provisions for political reservation for the Scheduled Castes and the Scheduled Tribes which is mandatory. Although when the provisions were made mandatory in 1950, it was decided that this would apply only for ten years and since then, the Constitution has been amended every ten year and political reservation for the Scheduled Castes and the Scheduled Tribes were extended. At present, there are 120 reserved parliamentary constituencies including 79 for the Scheduled Castes and 41 for the Scheduled Tribes in the country. Regarding the provisions for political reservations, Andre Betellie observes, "I think the general idea is that these should not be written into the Constitution permanently that in some future time the need for these special provisions will no longer exist. But that future seems to be moving further and further away. So that is political reservations." Along with this, the provisions for reservation for certain number of seats for the Scheduled Castes and the Scheduled Tribes in parliament and state assemblies, in government jobs and its gradual extension after every ten years is viewed by some as an attempt to create a permanent division in the society on caste lines.

NATIONAL COMMISSION FOR SCHEDULED CASTES AND SCHEDULED TRIBES

Another attempt under the special provisions relating to certain backward classes was setting up of the National Commission for Scheduled Castes and Scheduled Tribes. "The main aim of setting up this commission is attending to the grievances relating to service matters, exploitation, harassment as well as to ensure proper and just implementation of several acts, orders and instructions of the Union Government for safeguarding the interests of the SC/ST Community." Article 338 of the Constitution mentions," There shall be a Commission for the Scheduled Castes and Scheduled Tribes to be known as the National Commission for the Scheduled Castes and Scheduled Tribes. It shall be the duty of the Commission, (a) to investigate and monitor all matters relating to the safeguards provided for the Schedules Castes and Scheduled Tribes under this Constitution or under any other law of the time being in force or under any order of the Government and to evaluate the working of such safeguards; (b) to inquire into specific complaints with respect to the deprivation of rights and the safeguards of Scheduled Castes and Scheduled Tribes; (c) to present to the President, annually and at such other times as the Commission may deem fit, reports upon the working of those safeguards; (d) to discharge such other functions in relation to the protection, welfare and development and advancement of the Scheduled Castes and Scheduled Tribes as the President may, subject to the provisions of any law made by the Parliament, by rule specify."

The Scheduled Castes and Scheduled Tribes Commission has deep implications for the weaker sections. The Commission is vested with the constitutional powers mentioned below:

(a) Summoning and enforcing the attendance of any person from any part of India and examining him an oath;

(b) Requiring the discovery and production of any documents;

(c) Requisitioning any public record or copy thereof from any court or office; issuing Commission for the examination of witnesses and documents.

The first Report of the Commission was submitted to the President of India on 15th August, 1994. The Commission has handled 7918 complaints and petitions. It also made 44 field enquiries in reported case of atrocities on the people belonging to the Scheduled Castes and Scheduled Tribes. The National Commission for Scheduled Castes and Scheduled Tribes has 17 field offices under its control which provide, contact points with the state government and the field. They have been serving and providing assistance to the Commission in its various activities and various types of cases of complaints and representations and offences involving SC/ST. They also conduct inspection and evaluation of ongoing welfare projects run by the NGOs with assistance from the Government of India. The Commission has made a number of recommendations to protect and promote their interest and to move the society towards egalitarianism.

But the National Commission members implementation of statutory provisions for protection of the weaker sections, Mr. Dalip Singh Bhuria and other members of the Commission have lamented, "Even after 50 years (of independence) things have not improved." There is lack of proper infrastructure like roads and hospitals, the percentage of acquittals in cases of atrocities against SC and STs is as high as 95 per cent, lack of awareness about the provisions of the laws enshrined for protection of these communities.

The Commission has been unable to control assaults on the Dalits and the Tribals and to end the sufferings of the weaker section. Moreover, the appointments to it is political in nature, and they are inclined to follow their political party at the political establishment. Many a times the person losing in elections is accommodated within it. Due to these and many other shortcomings, the Commission has failed to be effective in practice.

A FUTURE COURSE OF ACTION

Yet, despite constitutional guarantees and welfare schemes the Scheduled Castes (SCs) and the Scheduled Tribes (STs) who are nearly a quarter of the Indian population have not improved considerably. The prejudice against them is present in form or another. "There has, in general, been an inherent lack of interest and seriousness on the part of the planning and implementing machinery to achieve the objectives of the Constitution . . . benefits secured by the SCs and STs do not appear commensurate with the funds spent so far." The representation of SCs and STs in the higher level of public service remains dismal, despite of reservation quota in jobs.

Until 1997, India has one of the largest experience of reservations but the results have been minimal. It exists and continues mainly for targeted electoral gains for politicians. Reservations has become imperative due to vote bank politics.

It is necessary to review the benefits of reservations in the past 60 years. The basis of making caste as the only criteria to identify the needy should be reviewed. A suggestion put forth can be a gradual reduction in the reservation quota by 2 per cent per annum at all levels and places; so as to ensure that reservations finally ends.

All these measures and ideals enshrined in the Constitution are aimed at bringing about change and has introduced a sense of awareness amongst the downtrodden. These downtrodden segments have begun to assert their right not only in the economic sphere but also social sphere where they were placed at the lowest levels of social hierarchy. These specific provisions are made to improve the status of these people socially and educationally, so that they can acquire a rightful place in the mainstream of the society. Specific efforts are made by the government to enable them to participate fully in the national development activities and has implemented several schemes pertaining to the socio-economic development of the SC/ST segment of population.

Although reservations cannot be panacea to all the problems that were faced by the SCs and STs. Prof. Ramesh Chandra remarks, "Reservations were never aimed at eliminating all ills of highly structured, hierarchical iniquitous Indian society, and not will, if eliminate all these in future. It, however, provides opportunities to Dalits in organized employment and produces a section capable of guiding and leading the community to emancipation." If the Dalits are brought into a dignified and rightful position through reservation, it is definitely going to boost economy and polity.

These measures will also have a positive effect on their lives although a lot more needs to be done in this field. With the passage of time, their problems have become multi-faceted which will not be solved by merely reservations. The debate on reservations has no relevance until the nation changes its mindset towards the downtrodden segment of our society. The fact is that the caste feelings still persists in the Indian society which is detrimental to an egalitarian approach. The hierarchical stratification in India have survived for centuries and they continue to be politically relevant and misused for the electoral gains.

So, the real challenge for the state is make these competititive through raising their standard so that their position is at par with the traditionally successful upper classes.

It is imperative to provide quality and standard and basic education to every section of out society. Instead of providing reservations to some castes and classes, the under-privileged sections should be made competent through education in getting a seat in monitories institutions through merit. This will make out nation progressive and a champion of the cause of the discriminated lot.

We must strive to provide a level playing field for all, where merit counts and reservations and such other amenliorative measures can be used only as a temporary measure. Our basic aim to is achieve an egalitarian society, where every individual has fair chances of their growth, access to educational and employment benefits and live a dignified and respectful life.

CHAPTER 9

The Issue of Women Reservation in India

The discussion for women's rights and issues have always been a subject of serious debate among the intelligensia and policy makers. Inequality between men and women is one of the most crucial disparities in our society. There is extensive discrimination against the women in the society, which violates the principles of equality of rights and respect for human dignity, which is an obstacle to the participation of women on equal terms with the men in society. This serves as an impediment to their growth and prosperity of the society. Women is considered as a weaker sex in society and that is why we talk about rights and protection of rights of women, so employment are not independent of each other. The women will be facilitated only when she is able to exercise her rights in socio-economic sphere.

With the 73rd Amendment Act, social dimensions like equity and egalitarianism have been injected into the political governance of the country. Yet, it might take a long time before the women of this country will get improved to fight against the evils and injustice meted out to them.

The areas of concern for women are growing violence against women at different levels of society, increasing dysfunctionality of the family, of legal machinery and its training systems, changing cultural norms, criminalization of politics, communalization of politics, etc. The women continue to be the oppressed in the society reinforced by the religious and social forces. All festivals and rituals perpetuate slavery and bondage of women. Women especially of the poor are particular victims of violence and social injustice, perpetuated in the name of caste, language and religion.

Of course, there has been a conscious articulation of women's issues in the past few decades especially amongst the urban and educated middle class. These women have organized themselves into movement and have lobbied and protested against blatant forms of discrimination that they face in our society. The experience of women's movement is a manifestation of collective struggle of women for justice and against corrupt and ruthless power hierarchy, having a definite bias for men in the society who have perpetuated subordination and exploitation of women.

HISTORICAL PERSPECTIVE

During the ancient historical period, there are reference to women's contribution to excellence in various fields including education, economy, politics, fine arts etc. The Vedic period is considered as the golden age of Indian womanhood. The status of women declined with the invasions on India. The evils of the nineteenth century namely purdah, widow oppression, Sati and other barbaric practices were the result of invasions.

Many restrictions were put on women biologically, culturally and socially and they were confined in the name of security, resulting in contraction of the role, capacity and contribution by women, declining their social power and familial status.

The onset of British rule, further aggravated their subordination and equality of women especially in the lower classes and castes. The factors responsible for this were changes in land ownership pattern, western oriented education, commercialization of economy, colonial rule etc. Nivedita Menon remarks, "The political economy of colonial rule had a specific impact on women because of new developments like lower wages, exclusion from some sectors which had been open to women before, and loss of usufructory rights to community property and resource through forest laws and the introduction of private property in land."

During the social reform movement attempts were made to improve the position of women by addressing the issues like child marriage, widow-remarriage, devdasi system, sati, polygamy etc. A few legal reforms were also introduced by British, with a few legislation passed against Sati, Widow remarriage etc.

In the context of constitutional reforms in the 1930s, legislative reservations for women were discussed. By this time separate electorate for Muslims, Sikhs and Christians were introduced and allocation of seats were done for depressed classes. During this period, organizations like All India Women's Congress (AIWC), the National Council of Women of India, Women's India Association etc. opposed legislative reservations for women on the ground that "to seek any form of preferential treatment would be to violate the integrity of the universal demand of Indian women for absolute equality of political status." While, Begum Shah Nawaz Khan who represented India at the First Round Table Conference in 1930, asserted that the women required special representation. Sarojini Naidu, who was a participant in the Second Round Table Conference in 1931, also opposed to reservation for women, even for orthodox Hindu and Muslim women.

The Government of India Act of 1935 provided provision for forty-one reserved seats in the provincial legislatures along with limited reservations in Central legislatures. The AIWC which initially opposed the constitutional provisions took advantage of it. In the 1937 elections, total fifty-six women became legislators, out of which forty-one were form the reserved seats, ten were from the unreserved and five were form nominated seats.

The Indian National Movement was an important mobilizer of women. Mahatma Gandhi's contribution in bringing women into politics is well-acknowledged. "The two central symbols that Gandhi used to generate a new life in the anti-imperialist struggle, khadi and salt were both explicitly derived from women's life-sustaining activities in the 'private' realm linking them in a revolutionary manner to the 'public'." During the Salt March through many villages, Sarojini Naidu was the first to join, who inspired hundreds of women to join the protest." Many women not only made salt, but also sat openly in market places selling and buying salt.

The nationalist movement was converted into mass movement and women took active participation in Civil Disobedience Movement, Quit India Movement, Swadesi, Boycott Movement, Home Rule Movement etc. Gandhi also championed the cause of liberation of women. He ardently espoused the cause of eliminating evils like purdah, prostitution, child marriage, oppression of widows, polygamy etc. Women again participated in Khadi Movement, other constructive programmes and educational and social reform movements to improve their status and to remove disabilities like backwardness, dependency, illiteracy, subordination etc. Moreover, women's organizations were constituted under the umbrella and control of the Congress party i.e. the Mahila Congress and the All India Women's Federation (CPI).

CONSTITUTIONAL AND LEGAL STATUS OF WOMEN

The Constitution of India provides equality to the Indian women:

(i) The Preamble to the Constitution in the objectives mentioned the constitutional status of women. It mentions:

Justice, social, economic and political,

Equality, of status and opportunity,

And to promote among them all fraternity assuring the dignity of the individual.

(ii) The Articles on Fundamental Rights elaborates upon:

- Article 14 ensures that the state shall not deny to any person equality before the law or the equal protection of the laws.
- Article 15 prohibits discrimination on grounds of religion, race, caste, sex or place of birth.
- Article 15(3) gives power to the state to make special provisions for women and children. This provision authorizes the state to make enactments for the welfare of women.
- Article 16 provides for the equality of opportunity in matters relating to public appointment.
- Article 17 declares the abolition of untouchability treating at par both men and women.
- Article 21A ensures the Fundamental Rights of compulsory education to every child up to the age of 14 years, which even a girl child, is also entitled to. This right incorporated through 86th Amendment Act and if executed with all earnestness and sincerity, would, indeed, pave the way for dignified and respectful life for the Indian women.
- Article 23 prohibits traffic in human beings, which includes prohibition of prostitution or immoral traffic in women and girls and also the system of devdasis.

(iii) The chapter on Directive Principle of State Policy, which provides direction to the state for the upliftment and welfare of all citizens, also provides for women-specific directives to;

- Men and Women equally have the right to an adequate means to livelihood. (Article 399)
- There is equal pay for equal work for both men and women (Article 39D)
- Health and strength of workers, men and women, and the tender aged children are not abused and

that citizens are not forced by economic necessity to enter vocation unsuited to their age or strength (Article 39E)

- The state has also been directed to provide for just and human conditions of work and maternity relief (Article 42)
- Part IVA of Constitution incorporated through 42nd Constitution Amendment Act, specifically declares that it shall be duty of every citizen to renounce practices derogatory to the dignity of women. (Article 51A-E)

(iv) Moreover, Article 325 ensures universal adult franchise and declares that no person shall be ineligible for inclusion in, or to claim to be included in a special, electoral roll on grounds of religion, race, caste or sex.

(v) Other legal provision is that Constitution guaranteed equal protection to all under the law and equal opportunities in public employment and prohibited discrimination in public places.

In the first decades of independence, various attempts were made to create new social institutions and to establish equality before law through reforms in the Hindu Family Law. In the years, 1955 and 1956, the Hindu Marriage Act, 1955 (later amended in 1964), the Hindu Adoption and Maintenance Act, 1956 (later amended in 1962), the Hindu Minority and Guardianship Act, 1956, and the Hindu Succession Act, 1956 were enacted.

The Parliament has enacted laws from time to time, has introduced progressive reform for the welfare of women and included specific provisions for the primary education, maternity benefits, share in property, equal remuneration etc. and for the removal of discrimination against women in matter concerning marriage, divorce, succession, maintenance, adoption, guardianship etc.

ATTITUDE TOWARDS WOMEN RESERVATIONS

The Committee of the Status of Women in India (CSWI) was appointed by the Government of India in 1971 with the objective to examine the Constitutional, legal, administrative provisions that have a bearing on the social status of women, their education and employment and to assess the impact of these provisions.

The impact of the marginalization process was first documented by CSWI in its much acclaimed report 'Towards Equality'. The report observes, "Every legal measure designed to translate the constitutional norms of equality or special protection into practice has had to face tremendous resistance from the legislature and other elites. We are, therefore, forced to observe that all the indicators of participation, attitudes and impact come up with the same results, the resolution in social and political status of women for which constitutional equality was to be the only instrument, still remains a very distant objective. . . . From this point of . . . the three recognized dimensions of inequality: Inequality of class/economic situation), status (social position) and political power. The review of the disabilities and constraints on women, which stem from the socio-cultural institutions, indicated that the majority of women are still very far from enjoying the rights and opportunities guaranteed to them by the Constitution. . . . The social laws, that sought to mitigate the problems of women in this country, who are as ignorant of their legal rights today as they were before independence."

In its probing interactions with the women, the committee although found that women's lack of political equality and the issue of the low participation of women in elected bodies were a major agenda with the women, but to disagreement within its own members (with Vina Mazumdar and Lotika Sarkar registering their dissent), the CSWI did not press upon the recommendations of reservations for women in the legislatures. The majority of Committee members considered reservations as "retrograde step from the equality conferred by the Constitution, and anticipated that such a system of special representation may precipitate similar demands from various other communities and interests that threaten national integration." However, the Committee urged for greater participation in the political institutions especially at the grassroots level and recommended the establishment of statutory women's panchayats at the local level."

The unanimous recommendation of the Committee was establishment of statutory women's panchayats and at the same time, also recommended that there should be no reservations in legislative assemblies and parliament. The arguments which were made in favour of reservations were, (a) Parties were reluctant to sponsor women candidates because of the overall patriarchal character of Indian politics, (b) Reservations would increase the number of women at one go and the inhibitions arising from their minority status would disappear faster, leading to increase in political participation, and (c) presence of more women in legislatures would lead to changes in direction of debates and policy. The arguments against reservations included: (a) women cannot be equated to socially backward communities as women are not a socially homogeneous group, (b) Women's interests could not be isolated from those of other economic and social strata, and (c) such a measure would lead to demands from other groups communities which could pose a threat to national integration."

Vina Mazumdar discussing on this issue, says, "Commenting on the failure of the state to disseminate the constitutional and other legal rights of women to the wider public, the CSWI had emphasized the need for some new institutional innovation, particularly in rural areas. Nothing that the provisions of one or two seats in panchayats, generally filled by nomination, had proved to be only a'tokenist' measure, notorious for this violation, the committee recommended statutory elected women's panchayat which would, (a) provide an agency to bring providing to the needs of women and children and (b) eliminate the practice of nominated members on the general panchayats, by bringing in the president and secretary of the women's body as genuine representatives of women to the general panchayats. The recommendations went into cold storage because of non-response from state governments."

THE ISSUE OF QUOTAS

In January 1985, Rajiv Gandhi government gave priority to the women's issues. A few official within the Ministeries of Social Welfare who had responsibility for Women's and Children's Welfare and Development, Rural Development and Labour and Employment, thought it "an opportune movement to reopen the debates on, (a) women's panchayats; and (b) widening opportunities for organizations of poor rural women-through assistance for economic activities taken up collectively. Some programmes were initiated by all the three ministries demonstrating a convergence of approach which as welcomed by several women's organizations."

But, during 1986, the Muslim Women's (Protection of Rights on Divorce) Act, 1986 and Deorala Sati incident in 1987 were a severe blow to gender equality. In this changed political climate, the women felt certain annoyance. Hence, the Government of India constituted a core group to draft a National Perspective Plan (NPP), which submitted its report in 1988. A proposal of the draft of NPP suggested the introduction of 30 per cent reservation to be introduced at all levels of elective bodies, to be filled by nomination/co-option in the initial stages. This was opposed and "provoked universal condemnation as subversion of the Constitution and democratic process." The women organizations rejected this principle and insisted that reservations should be restricted to the panchayat and other local governmental institutions, to be filled through elections," giving due representation to the Scheduled Castes, Scheduled Tribes and the poor section of women. The NPP recommended 33 per cent reservation for women of the seats in all elected assemblies from village to Union level and suggested that political parties should promote women's electoral representation by allotting at least 33 per cent of their tickets to women. Since the report of NPP women was published many organizations had intensified the demand for increased participation of women in politics.

RESERVATIONS IN PANCHAYATS

The idea of making a legal provision of reserving seats for women the Parliament and State Assemblies and other decision-making bodies at the highest level, started gaining firm grounds during the tenure of Rajiv Gandhi, as the Prime Minister of India. Grassroots democracy were strengthened, when the Panchayat Raj Act, 1992 (73rd and 74th Constitutional Amendments) created new democratic institutions of local governance. These Amendments granted not less than one-third reservation to women in the Panchayat Raj Institutions or the local bodies. As a result, by 1999, approximately 7,68,582 women had been elected to Gram Panchayat, 38,582 women to Panchayat Samities and 4030 women were elected at the Zila Parishad level.

Although it is commonly agreed that even this reservation principle was not adequate at the local level and had many practical drawbacks and was not adequate to provide empowerment to the women. But it provided opportunity to the women for their empowerment. Niraja Gopal Jayal emphasizes on the fact that "women representatives give greater priority to issues such as drinking water supply, installation of parks, playgrounds, roads, community infrastructure, schooling etc. A vocal section of women have been mobilized at social and political level at the grassroots level, started understanding the system of governance at the local level. These women are attempting to challenge the feudal basis of the family. They now constitute the local leaders who enjoy mass following and have been a part and parcel of the mass struggles going in their areas, yet never have been granted the opportunity and power to challenge the system from within. The women movement has been broadened and given impetus to their election. Women Sarpanchs and panchayat members who were able to wield enough authority, have changed their decision of panchayats in favour of women. Women leaders are increasingly taking on the role of champion of the women's cause, raising pertinent issue improving the status of women."

The participation of women in panchayats has given rise to new developmental priorities and has enriched gender-friendly governance. It has changed the lives of numerous women in the countryside and has created conditions for their equal participation in local government. The patriarchal attitudes prevalent in the society and family, denial of formal education to women etc. were the biggest deterrents to their political participation. Reservation of women in Panchayati Raj Bodies (PRIs) came as a way to ensure conditions not only for gender equality in the political sphere but also a pivotal role in the empowerment and socio-economic upliftment of women. This has encouraged more and more women into the political arena. Mani Shankar Aiyer, Panchayat Raj Minister calling it "an extraordinary act of social and political empowerment" said, commented, "We have approximately 12 lakh women in the panchayat alone. As against the reserved quota of 33 per cent, their actual presence ranges around 38 per cent. This means that not only are we easily able to find women candidates to contest some 12 lakh posts but also there is on an average three or four contestants for a post. This means that approximately 50 lakh or 5 million women have been liberated from the kitchen and the courtyard and brought into the public domain. This is an extraordinary act of social and political empowerment."

Since the experiment at the Panchayat level has been encouraging, it laid the grounds of serious efforts to build broad-based consensus for providing equitable representation to women in Parliament and legislative assemblies. This enhanced participation and emergence of women leadership at the level of local self-government prepared grounds for their participation at various levels. It has opened doors for women belonging to various sections especially the under-privileged groups. So, the instances of women succeeding as Panchayat leaders have made a strong case of reservation of seats for them in the legislatures.

RESERVATIONS IN PARLIAMENT AND LEGISLATIVE ASSEMBLIES

The state is committed towards ensuring "progressively the full and equal participation of women in all for and process of the decision-making both at the level of policy-making and that of implementation in all sectors including legislative, executive and judicial institutions. The ultimate target should be to achieve complete parity between women and men in all decision-making bodies." The popular demand was to have a more equitable representation to women in parliament and legislative assemblies. This issue has mobalized the women explicitly across the country over a past decade and more and mentioned in memorandum at the state and Central levels, in discussions, workshops, discussions etc. Indu Agnihotri senior fellow at the Centre for Women's Studies, says, "The demand was a logical continuation of what had been achieved relatively easily at the level of local representatives bodies after the adoption of the 73rd-74th Amendments to the Constitution in 1993."

In 1995, the question of quotas was raised, again this time the focus was women in Parliament. It was argued that women representation the Parliament is meant to bring forth many specific problems pertaining to oppression of women, which cut across caste lines and religious communities. Prime Minister H.D. Dev Gowda made the actual promise for reservation of seats for women in Parliament and State Assemblies in 1996. I.K. Gujral proposed the present from and shape of the Bill during his tenure as the Prime Minister of India. When the Bill addressing this issue was introduced in the Eleventh Parliament in 1997, several parties and groups raised objections.

The objectives focused around two main issues, first the issue of overlapping quotas for women in general and those for the women of the lower castes and second, the issue of elites. Most women's group felt that the caste issue was a divisive one for women. Many even felt uneasy about giving special privileges to the elite women by ensuring seats for them in the Parliament, although they had previously supported quotas for women at the grass-roots level of the panchayats.

In the year 1998, there was a mass protest before Parliament with a massive participation of almost 10,000 women pressing their demands in New Delhi.

A slightly modified version, the Constitution (Eighty-fifth Amendment) Bill, 1999, was introduced in the Lok Sabha on 23 December, 1999, with no discussion allowed for the MPs tore the Bill each time when it was listed for discussion. Justice Rajinder Sachar says that "History is been repeated every year. Parliament is the matter of hypocrisy of all political parties in the context of the Women Reservation Bill." Every time the Bill is presented, "And then a force rather than a tragedy is played out by so-called radical politicians, jumping into the well of the House, tearing copies of the Bill and making impossible for proceeding to continue, the House gets adjourned, the Bill is thrown into the dust bin till it is revived in subsequent years with the same result. It is time this mockery stopped, considering that the Congress, the BJP and Left parties proclaim that they are for the Bill in the present form and really want it to become a law."

The Bill in its current form envisages reserving almost 180 seats in the Parliament for women. Also, there is a provision of a rotation of seats, i.e. a male member of Parliament cannot represent the same constituency for more than two consecutive terms. Rajinder Sachar anticipates the problems of this provision on the grounds "that the reservation of seats for women would mean rotation of seats at every general elections with the result that the members will not be able to nurse their constituencies and also that candidates will be uncertain of anticipating their future constituencies."

It is true with the agenda of women's emancipation taking centre stage of political arena and with women asserting as an independent social force, no political party can dare to directly oppose the bill providing for one-third reservation of women in the elected houses of the people. Almost all the Prime Ministers of India and Lok Sabha leaders in the past decades have fielded questions from women representatives on the issue. The assertion of women has also manifested itself in the opposition of women MPs on the question of referring the bill to a joint select committee in the name of quota for women in Rajya Sabha, legislative council and for oppressed castes, etc., postponing the actual constitutional amendment for discussion in the subsequent session.

Many contradictory reactions have emerged on the Women's Quota Bill from time to time.

While Uma Bharati has defied the BJP's official party position, put forward by Atal Behari Vajpayee, saying OBCs should be granted reservation too and that it would be better to have 33 per cent reservation for women, 33 per cent for men (SC, ST and OBC) and the rest in the general category. Meera Kumar and Shailja have also voiced their concern over SC and ST quota, opposing the bill in its present form. Although stalwarts like Pramilla Dandavate and Margaret Alva have gone on record saying that 33 per cent reservation will go a long way in paving the way for women's emancipation. Margaret Alva has targeted the male representatives in the 11th Lok Sabha, saying that they have a political vested interest in not allowing 180 seats to slip out of their hands. 180 seats in Parliament is too great a number to be sacrificed for the mere ideal of women's empowerment or adequate political representation, the very idea makes the male politicians panicky.

The entire exercise of supporting or opposing the bill has brought into sharp contradiction the women's position with official party positions. It has also exposed the fact that though the bill cannot be opposed, the remnants of feudal mindset within parties as well as their apprehensions about the danger of such reforms having strategic implications—which may drastically affect party policies, especially those relating to women, in a situation where women have hardly been accorded equal status and position within these parties—remain quite real. For example, much before the bill had been tabled Phoolan Devi of the Samajwadi Party had gone on record saying, "Only by guaranteeing 50 per cent reservation for women right from the Panchayat level upto the Lok Sabha can the lot of women be improved." Poolan Devi a lower caste MP also presented reservations against women's Representation Bill because women with "short hair and lipstick" would get in Parliament, while OBC women would not. Our (OBC) women are uneducated and cannot understand anything so unless there is reservation for them they cannot come to Parliament."

Yet the political mentor of Phoolan, Mulayam Singh Yadav faced the charge of engineering an attack on the life of the erstwhile woman Chief Minister of UP, Ms. Mayawati in the Guest House incident, which Phoolan found hard to defend. Not only this, neither Phoolan nor Mayawati were able to defend their parties' role in the Muzaffarnagar rape case. Or, for that matter, although Margaret Alva accorded credit to the Rajiv Gandhi regime for initiating the process of empowering women at the panchayat level or regarded Indira Gandhi as the ultimate example of women power, it is the Congress ideology that was visible when Congress(I) MP Ajit Jogi vehemently opposed the move for introducing the 81st Amendment by saying "this is not the kind of affirmative action which will help women. My apprehension is that it will destroy the strongest link in Indian society—that is, the family. The housewife or the mother is the pivot around which the entire family revolves and if they go after these offices, the family will be neglected."

On the other hand, the CPI-CPI(M) has the policy to support progressive reforms in favour of women and their leaders certainly support the 81st Amendment Bill in their own way. So, the leader of the CPI(M) women's wing, Ms. Brinda Karat says, 'Reservation should not only be quantity based but also quality based' and takes of poor women having more in common with poor men than the rich women'. Yet it is a well known fact that the police officer responsible for inflicting inhuman torture to the pro-Naxal, Ms. Archana Guha was rewarded and promoted by the CPI(M) government and only after years of struggle that he was now been awarded a token punishment of one year imprisonment and a fine. Archana was not a lone fighter but stands as the representative of hundreds of women activists and supporters of the Naxalite movement in West Bengal, the struggle of the poorest of poor. Even the powerful parties like Rashtriya Janata Dal (RJD), Samata Samajwadi Party (SP) and Bahujan Samaj Party (BSP) opposed the Bill and contend that elite upper caste women will monopolize reserved seats because they are better educated.

There are many such example of the double speak of political leaders of the 'established' political parties. These are the political parties which have perpetrated or abetted the most heinous of crimes against women and repressed even the most feeble voice of assertion for women—some have even used rape and public humiliation of women as a weapon against the dalits, the lower backward castes, the minorities and tribals.

In BJP, the most ardent supporter of this bill was Atal Behari Vajpayee, the Prime Minister who remained in office for thirteen days only who made haste to declare reservation for women, and sought to push a private bill on the issue and, till the end, stuck to passing the bill in its present form. Though the party claims the maximum number of women MPs and appointment of a woman as its national spokesperson, the anti-women antecedents of BJP are quite obvious. It was Murli Manohar Joshi, of the BJP who termed the Beijing Conference for women as an open invitation to sexual promiscuity and a platform for legitimizing abortion rights, childbirth out of wedlock or single motherhood. He has gone on to glorify the feudal basis of the 'ideal Indian family' and the subjugation of woman in the name of a glorious tradition of the 'ideal Indian woman'—tolerance, compassion and harmony—which was worth emulating the world over.

THE QUESTION OF RESERVATION FOR WOMEN IN GOVERNMENT JOBS

A next step to reservations in Parliament and Legislative Assemblies, there is also talk of reservation for women in government jobs. This provision has to address a larger cross-section of the women population. This provision is likely to create furore in the society. Although, it will be more difficult to realize in practice due to many factors like feudal pressures existing in the family, lack of child care and maternity health facilities, responsibility for the aged and education of children etc. Another factor is also that employment for women raises the question of the nature of work and working conditions.

Tedious and mundane jobs, stereotyping 'women's vocations' and negligence of the state on the question of women's health are big deterrents to the enthusiasm and urge of women themselves and also serve as excuses for families to keep women out of work. And further, there has evolved no means to ensure equal say in the economic decision-making within the family, not to speak of families being run on the women's income while the man's income remains solely under his personal control. The other facet is reservation creating social tensions in a situation where jobs are already shrinking and crores of men still remaining unemployed.

Hence, the reservations in other spheres like education, private institutions and political parties entails long years of struggle in a male-dominated society. At present, despite strong and widespread women movement, the highest representation of women was merely 9 per cent in the Lok Sabha in 1999 and 15.4 per cent in Rajya Sabha in 1991. Infact, in the year 2005, the percentage reduced to 8.2 and 11.4 respectively.

THE ISSUE OF CASTE SUB-QUOTAS

Some thinkers are of the view that goal of an inclusive society can be achieved only with sub-quotas for the marginalized groups amongst women.

Some political leaders have raised the issue for a sub-quota for Muslim women also. However, a sub-quota for Muslim women would be violative of the provisions of secularism, a basic feature of the Constitution.

Another major problem is the demand raised by the backward caste leaders for a caste sub-quota in the women's quota. The caste system is so deeply entrenched in the Indian psyche that unless some drastic measures are taken the women belonging to backward tribes will remain excluded and isolated from the mainstream. Empowerment through reservation in political bodies will go a long way in addressing their isolation, exclusion and oppression.

The data of representation of OBC women in various bodies is almost negligible. The data of representation of Dalit women in parliament is an indicator of this. A special mechanism has to be developed to ensure that these women have their share and participation by resorting to quota. The past records show that political parties have not given much space to Dalit women in proportion to their population share. In 1971, of the total Scheduled Castes members of Parliament, only 1.56 per cent were women whereas they constitute half of the Scheduled Caste population. Between 1971 and 1991, it remained between 4.94 per cent to 6.41 per cent. Their numbers have increased to 13 per cent in 1996 and in 2004, again, their share remained 13 per cent only.

The alternative suggested is that there should be quotas within the political parties itself. But, most of the political parties, which are supposed to work for other backward castes, are generally under-represented in the parliament. So, as a result, even if some share is given to backward classes women, they will remain unrepresented.

Some feel the only way to ensure representation is through earmarking specific number of seats in proportion to some agreed criterion, preferably population. Unless there is a special provision like quota within the quota for dalit women, they will remain sidelined and be left behind in the process of political empowerment. It is also necessary to recognize that the OBC women are at the bottom of the social structure and constitute the most poverty stricken, neglected and marginalized section of the society, hence deserve representation.

So, parties like Rashtriya Janata Dal, the Samajwadi Party etc. want the Women Reservation Bill to include a sub-quota for Other Backward Classes (OBCs) and Muslim women on the grounds that otherwise, the quotas will only promote the interests of the elite.

Zoya Hasan discusses the whole issue of the caste sub-quota in the women's quota at length and believes that women's quotas will not unfavourably affect OBC women. She remarks, "The most strident opposition to women's quotas has come from the lower caste legislators and politicians who fear that their political concerns would be but at risk. They worry that women's reservation will slacken the lower caste challenge to upper caste domination. According to them, women's quotas are a means to re-establish the monopoly of the upper caste because they will cover the benefits of quotas. They, therefore, demand a sub-quota within the women's quota for lower caste women. There is, however, no major conflict between gender and caste, indeed, quotas are likely to facilitate the entry of women from all castes and communities into legislatures. Unlike caste quotas, women's quotas will not alter caste equations. They will change male-female equations and give greater opportunity to women to contest elections. That is why parties would have to find suitable candidates from the same castes for seats currently held by OBC members. In other words, women's quotas will not unfavourably affect OBC women, rather, they are more likely to get elected under this system than otherwise. If anything, the women reservation bill will act as a source of further advantage, as it has done for Muslim women in the local bodies even in the absence of reservations.

Another argument for not favouring such a quota is the even without reservation OBC men have managed to gain entry into the state legislatures and Parliament, and the same can be applied to the women as well. The OBC-dominated constituencies, the political parties especially the lower caste parties give tickets to the OBC women and even without quotas, women from these groups have managed to win more legislative seats. For example, in Bihar, out of ten women MLA's five belonged to the OBC, two each to the SC, ST and only one from the upper caste.

However, "The OBC leaders rationalize the lowering of the women's quota on the grounds of scarcity of experienced women. They argue that it would be difficult to find so many women contestants for legislative seats." Many women in organizations have criticised this proposal as a "compromise formula" on the grounds that it will only ensure tickets but not seats for women.

THE QUESTION OF POLITICAL PARTICIPATION

There had been suggestions in the past in the form of alternatives to the Bill. One is to amend the Representation of People's Act 1951, to compel political parties to nominate women for one-third of their seats or lose recognition.

The Election Commission has proposed another alternative which requires a compulsory quota for women in party nominations. It recommend that all political parties are required to field women in at least one-third of their seats in every state for Parliament and also one-third seats in each region of the state for the state assemblies. The parties failing to do this would lose the Election Commission's recognition.

The objections against this proposal has been that it would not guarantee 33 per cent women winning elections, as parties may give relatively weaker seats within each state and district to women, resulting in their subsequent defeat. So, the new proposal is to give 10-15 per cent seats to women which received a better response and support of many parties and several small women's groups.

This, according to Rajindar Sachar, former Chief Justice, is flawed, as it would violate the Constitution of India, which guarantees its citizens the right to form association under Article 19(1)(c) as a fundamental right. Another alternative is to increase the number of seats in the Lok Sabha, which is currently based on the figures of the census of India, 1971, when the population of India was 54 crores. The numbers of seats were limited to 530 till further amendments. Now the Delimitation Commission has been asked to take the 2001 census as the basis for delimiting constituencies. According to 2001 census, the population of India has risen to 102 crores, therefore the number of seats are bound to increase before the next general elections. This should be reason enough to pave the way for the safe passage of the Women's Reservation Bill.

CONCLUSION

No nation can progress if it discriminates against any of its citizens. No society can be progressive society of the modern civilized world unless it treats its women at par with men. It is time to provide genuine and full empowerment of women. Women should be given due place in our society including our political institutions, our economic processes and every walk of life.

One of the key issues today is the empowerment of women. Women issues have received tremendous attention at all forums and platforms including national and global, although formulation and exertion of the policies has not changed the grassroots. The real test of democracy is the creation of equality of opportunity for the hitherto deprived section of the society. Ensuring political participation in the decision-making process is one of the mechanism through which we can engineer social change.

UNICEF's 'State of the World's Children Report 2007' advocates quotas for a greater political participation of women throughout the world and has proved to be an effective method for women's empowerment. The report also mentions that 'of the 20 countries with the largest number of women in Parliament, 17 countries are using quota is some form or the other. 'It is because of the reservations in panchayats, representation of women is one-third at the local legislatures although women members have only 10% representation in the Parliament. The women's representation in the Lok Sabha is merely 8.3% which is much lower than other Asian giants China (20.3%) and Pakistan (21.3%). Moreover, the representation of women in Lok Sabha has reduced from 9.6% in 1999 to 8.3% in 2004.

So, the report admits that quotas are not a panacea. "To be effective, quotas have to match the electoral system of a country, unless they do, and unless commitments are reinforced by a political system in which rules matter and failure to comply carries consequences, the role of quotas is merely symbolic. The report lays down seven milestones to achieve gender parity: education, financing, legislation, legislative quotas, women empowering women, engaging men and boys, and improved research and data."

It is our proud legacy that India's freedom struggle upheld women's rights. Mahatma Gandhi declared that as long as women of India did not take part of public life, there is no salvation for our country. Out Constitution is based on the idea of gender equality and the necessity to empower women.

We have to make conscious efforts to usher in a new era in which everyone in equal, irrespective of caste, creed, religion, gender or sex. We also have to correct every historic inequality, for the reservations become imperative. But introducing more and more unrealistic reservation policies and by wasting a lot of resources in the name of social justice by pulling back those who are surging ahead is not the only solution.

We have to reconsider our social empowerment strategies especially with reference to women. Providing special privileges or quotas would not provide a long lasting solution. We have to build a society by which dignified living in ensured, thereby safeguarding her privileges in the society. In fact, the struggle for a more egalitarian and humane path of development will take India on a forward path, not merely pressing for representation based on identity.

CHAPTER 10

Reservation in Private Sector and the Corporate Class

The discourse on reservation in the private sector began with the similar premise like that of the original reservations itself. Reservation is a mechanism to provide and ensure equality to the people who have remained oppressed socially and economically for a long period of time. It was socio-cultural disability of the Indian society to treat people from certain communities not on equal footing. The premise behind reservation was conceived, on the same basis as the premise behind reservations in the private sector. The correct premise behind the rationale of reservations is rearticulated and the premise behind reservations in the private sector is based on the argument, "it is a counter veiling measure by the state against the socio-cultural disability of the Indian society. "This disability does not restrict the domain of reservations of the state sector, but it pertains more to the civil society which should be enlightened enough to see the need for reservations. The premises behind reservations in the private sector can be considered as the belated addition of the original premise behind the reservations. It is a mechanism through which the rights of certain sections of the society are ensured because left to itself, the societal conditions will not allow them to exercise these rights. Reservations are to create self-confidence among the people, who through history, had been victims of the most heinous forms of discrimination. It is a form of positive discrimination to ensure equality to them and to claim their rightful position in a democratic society.

The private sector is not a homogenous unit and comprise of numerous enterprises, big and small. Since these units are not homogenous, most of the private sector companies have serious problems regarding their hiring policy. It is a common feature that a very few of them have a transparent system of recruitment. In most of the cases recruitment is done on the basis of 'network', which excludes certain people rather than discriminating against them. Regular advertisements for jobs in the private sector is not a commonly used mode of recruitment. The companies prefer the candidates who are recommended and generally, do not go into the open market, and since the backward sections are generally not recommended, they do not get the jobs. Dipankar Gupta comments, "So it is not as it SCs and STs are purposively discriminated against. Perhaps SCs and STs do not make it to the private sector because they lack those critical network connections. Otherwise, in a large number of major private companies, particularly the transnational and multinational, there is no real interest regarding the caste background of a person. . . . The rule of thumb for private sector recruitment in most cases is: no network connections, no jobs.'

Even the statistics show that informal and personalized channels are a preferred mode of recruitment. The workforce employed through those channels "formed more than 70 per cent in Pune (1959), 60 per cent in Mumbai (1976) and a equally high proportion in Ahmedabad (1975), Coimbatore (1986-87) and Surat (1998)."Because of indirect and backdoor reservations, there is a growing demand for same sort of affirmative action policy for the private sector which so far has remained outside the purview of any kind of anti-discriminatory measure and in which more than 90 per cent of the dalit and adivasi workforce in engaged.

Now-a-days, the private sector receives a huge financial assistance from the government while in proportion to this, they open up only a small percentage of jobs in the organized private sector to the marginalized sections. On the basis of merit and qualifications, they do not qualify to often jobs in the private sector.

Discrimination on the basis of religion, ethnicity, national, class, caste etc., exist in our social system. Sukhdeo Thorat says, "In order to correct the imbalances in terms of access to capital assets, employed, education, political participation and other spheres, countries have turned to practices of reservations, affirmative action, positive action or equal opportunity policies for these discriminated sub-groups along with pro-poor policies." Most of these policies and programmes of intervention operate in respect to sub-group populations identified by ethical, racial, religious or gender characteristics. The examples are not only from the West (USA, UK, Northern Ireland and Yugoslavia) but also from Latin American countries like Brazil, Bolivia, Peru, African countries like Nigeria, Sudan, South Africa and countries like Malaysia, Pakistan, China, Japan and India from Asia.

It is surprising that while the affirmative action policy in many of these countries was to began with use for both private and public sector, the Indian state never thought of bringing the private sector under the purview of a reservation policy-even though it is the past of discrimination in the private domain that led us to accept the reservation policy for the private sector."

A new lease of life was given to the issue of reservation when there was a debate to extend to the private sector. The public sector has contributed and given their due share, so now the private sector which was not a part to it should also "carry a part of it." In this concern, Andre Betellie strongly feels, "After all, the private and public sectors are both parts of the same society, and no major stake holder in it should remain indifferent to its well-being."

With the opening up of our economy and initiation of the policies of liberalization and globalization, in the 1990s, the public sector started receding and its place was taken by the private sector. The marginalized were unable to withstand in the changed atmosphere for the requisite skills to procure enough jobs was not present in them.

How and in what form, we need to extend the public sector reservations policy was discriminated groups in the private sector is the major area of concern. There is enormous experience of our own public sector reservation policy. The Indian state could also benefit from the measures used against discrimination in private sector of other countries in the world.

A HISTORICAL PERSPECTIVE

Inspired by the ideal to build nationalist solidarity and embracing the concept of social justice, senior Birla and Bajaj supported Gandhi's untouchability companion during the freedom struggle. Financial support was also given to Gandhi for the freedom struggle by various industrialists.

In the initial years of independence, the corporate class adopted a more skeptical rather than a hostile attitude towards the provisions for reservations. The reservations were considered the responsibility of the public sector. This class initially, having been spared the pressures of promoting and pushing social justice, members of this class built more temples than schools for dalits and children.

The reservations began in the right earnest only in the late 1960s and with it Dalits started barely entering the exclusive domain of the higher class. It was still the preponderance in clerical jobs, at the most only in Class IV that comprised the lowest jobs and included sweepers that the representation of dalits far exceeded the prescribed percentage. Needless to say, their presence in Class I post was nearly negligible.

Their entry in the job market, did not automatically obviate the caste oppression which they had been subjected from a long time. The reason is that dalits have to work to earn favour from their upper castes employers. "It is only through this process, they can reach positions of real position and in return be acknowledged as meritorious. The fact, however, remains that they are turned comprador to their community; while schizophrenically chanting about their dalit interests, they consciously and unconsciously serve their interests of the existing power structure."

The policy of reservations in government jobs for the SCs and STs, has to some extent guaranteed their participation in public employment. Different classes have achieved the benefits of reservations. Today the number of Dalits have increased in the Grade I services. As per the current estimates by Ministry of Statistics and Programme Implementation for the year 2002-03, the Dalits occupy a little more than 12 per cent of the Grade I in the public sector, although the proportion of Dalits in Grade I services remained somewhere around 1 per cent for the past fifty years. As we climb down the ladder, the number of Dalits keep on increasing till we reach the Grade IV level, where they are actually over-represented.

Also, statements by members of the present government relating to the extension of reservations to the private sector has once again brought the issue of reservations to the centre stage. In addition to the persisting concerns about distributive justice, affirmative action and quotas, they have raised serious problems. The Constitution makes provisions for reservation of seats in public employment. It left out the private domain, which is now being targeted and there is a even growing demand for reserving job for socially and economically backward class in the private sector.

With the opening up our economy and the initiation of the policies of liberalization and globalization in the 1990s, the opportunities in the public sector started reducing. Due to this the dalits and tribes who were not skilled enough to stay in the changed market scenario were affected badly. Even though the semi-skilled and skilled workers had a fair choice but still the majority of them are the suffering lot. The denial of job opportunities to the dalits on the grounds of merit and qualifications in the private sector, have made the demand of extension of reservation policy to the discriminated groups in the private sector as an area of women.

REACTION OF THE CORPORATE CLASS

The issue of reservations had received a mixed response from the corporate class ranging, from the most vociferous supporters to the strident critics. There is no denying that mandating job reservations in the private sector will have far-reaching consequences on jobs. The corporate sector is mainly concerned with performance and one's capability to deliver and it does not matter to them if a person is belongs to OBC category or not.

The corporate class has remained relatively skeptical on the issue of reservation. One of the leading journalist commented with anguish, "We would rather move out of Maharashtra, if the state government decides to implement the reservation policy in the private sector." They believe that inefficiencies will creep into the system, if we ignore meritocracy. The corporate class, so far, has been considering the caste as a liability rather than an asset and has an inherent bias that mostly favours the upper castes. In the recruitment process, there is a mutual disinterest, in appointing the backward castes. They also ardently espouse the cause of having reservations not on the grounds of caste. N.R. Narayana Murthy, Chairman and Chief, Infosys, says, "I'm not against reservations, but it should be based on economics and not caste. If a person is hampered by resources, I think those people should be given reservations."

Most of the industry leaders are not in favour of reservations, at least not on the basis of caste. Azim Premji, Wipro Chairman, on the issue of reservations said, "We appreciate the compulsions that the country in going through in terms of reservations but the only way we can compete with global players is by hiring best in class people from India and the rest of the world. We are an organization that require to select people on merit."

Of course, losided educational development has produced structural exclusion of dalits from highly prestigious institutions like IITs and other institutions, which provides them entry into the corporate sector. "In view of the structural denial of opportunities in the private sector and the lack of actual placement in a sphere other than the sanitary divisions, the demand for procedural and not simply protective justice, appear legitimate. Procedural justice, in turn demand a constitutionalization of reservation provisions in the private sector. However, this would be unacceptable to the corporate class for the following reasons. It poses a serious challenge to the autonomy of the corporate class, which finds constitutionalization and governmentalization as impinging on their generic rights to decide merit without any directive and dictation from the state."

The corporate class firmly believes that merit is the defining marker of the private sector and 'purity of merit' can be maintained only if quotas are not there in private sector for reservations provisions tend to produce only 'dumb' candidates. Arun Shourie, former disinvestment minister remarks, "Investment will be more uncertain in an increasingly competitive world, if jobs are given on the basis of my birth and not on the basis of my capability." This argument invariably referred to the 'reservation policy' that people would add to the salary bill and also, lower the standards of efficiency in organizations. Vikram Talwar, CEO, EXL services, after deliberating upon the repercussions of quota implementation in the private sector, says, "It's ludicrous. The entire industry will go down the drain. The dream of a multi-billion dollar business process outsourcing industry, forget about it." Today, India is being regarded as world's intellectual capital, so increasing reservations will not only hamper merit, but also make other countries suspect Indian talent. So, the corporate class has vehemently opposed the quota system could be disastrous not only for the future of the private sector but also for the Indian economy.

They argue that if they are allowed to perform without these constraints, as a normal private sector company would do, they will definitely demonstrate their entrepreneurial prowess and managerial competence. Rajeev Chandra Shekhar, Chief BPL Innovision comments, "Reservations will not increase job penetration for the lower sections. Industry is already disadvantaged with high cost, bureaucracy and delays. You cannot add one more and expect us to produce growth."

The move for job quotas in the private sector has come at a time when the Indian economy has begun to change its course. The state is relaxing its hold on the 'commanding heights' of the economy to give more room to the market so as to raise the rate of growth through increased competition. It is now realized that the Indian economy cannot do well nationally unless it becomes competitive internationally. Privatization, liberalization and globalization require an employment policy that is radically different from one governed by mandatory quotas based on caste and community. Without the replacement of a rigid and quota-based employment policy by an open and flexible one, the Indian economy cannot maintain the momentum given to it by the reforms started in 1991.

India, today is gaining firm grounds as knowledge economy and manufacturing hub. In such circumstances, India would be losing jobs and incur a huge loss to the industry. Sudhir Jalan, president of the All India Management Association (AIMA) agrees, "Today we're on the cusp of high growth, if the government keeps playing to the galleries, all that we're achieved will have to be sacrificed. We have to compete globally, if you have job quotas, how many MNCs will want to come to India?"

Many industries function on the basis of skilled human resource, and if such companies are compelled to employ a requisite number of their workforce from the backwards, it will definitely have an adverse impact on their performance. So, most of the companies are against any kind of mandatory reservations is a hindrance to scheme of merit based employment policy and will be a hindrance in employment of merit and skill in the industry.

In a sharp contrast, a relatively more enlightened section of the corporate class has taken a more *sympathetic* view of this. It is based on the corporate commitment to the issue of social justice and shown an inclination towards the affirmative action. The organizations pay their due to society and government in various ways and are prepared to "fund development" of the reserved classes, although according to their view it should be a reasonable way and not an imposition from the government. An insider, in this sense, remarks that "if government ties up our hand and feet, that's unfair." According to them, the corporate sector, in their pursuance of corporate social responsibility, already is addressing concerns of economically backward classes. CII President, R Seshasayee comments, "My company, Ashok Leyland is providing training to 20,000 and need not introduce compulsory quotas drivers a year. Also, the Tatas, Birlas, Dr. Reddy's, Thapars . . . every group is involved and is carrying out its social responsibility."

The supporters of this argument put forward that affirmative action programmes are endorsed by the corporate class in other countries like Malaysia etc. and even in our country, states like Tamil Nadu have implemented reservations, without any negative impact on the economy.

Underscoring the premise of the self-evident 'merit' argument that the influx of other backward castes will erode the 'merit', they argue that there could be people from these castes with requisite merit and capability. In the earlier times, people took the meaning of merit as the scholastic performance, academic rank, marks etc. It was apparently used against dalits in the beginning for they obviously lacked in these aspects. Yet, it is a fact that despite possessing these attributes, people from the oppressed communities are not successful in getting entry to the corporate sector. Reservations are taken as concessions extended with the intent of uplifting these low caste people to compensate the poor material and discriminatory social conditions that had been forced upon them.

Reservations cannot serve as an elixir for the inequalities in the society. "Reservations are like a bitter pill for some chronic disease, which cannot be perennially good for any body. Nobody likes to take bitter pills without reasons. Pills, however, can be stopped only after the disease is gone." The policy of reservations have to work in sync with the corporate class. If the upper class elites desires that reservations should go, they should come forward to work for removing the long remaining societal liability. The reservations are not in the interests of the Dalits either for it has "marred their rebellious zeal and co-opted them into the system." They have been deviated from their long-term emancipatory project of the annihilation of the castes.

It is a fact that reservation process in India has been instrumental in upward mobility of the downtrodden, but increasing reservations will hamper merit and quality. It must be kept in mind that correcting the historical wrongs does not create new wrongs. Reservations, in due course, will make the people take the things for granted rather than adopting a spirit of striving for the desired things in life. If the government decides to enhance the ambit of reservation to the corporate sector, it would have serious repercussions and dilute excellence and quality. So the policy of reservation must give way to a new way to reach the goal of emancipation and upliftment of communities and individuals.

Infact, individual companies are now-a-days, pursuing some policies on Corporate Social Responsibility voluntarily and are socially accountable in the interest of equity, fairness and justice. Affirmative action on reservation is a part of mature corporate governance. The companies are willingly following the policies encouraging the inclusion of all sections especially the backward ones which eventually has a positive influence on the company's market insight and its performance. Andre Betellie is very optimistic and companies, in due course, will been couraged to work upon a conducive formula introducing affirmative action programmes which is in their interest. He comments, "There is no reason why the better Indian companies should not take the lead in devising active affirmative action programmes for themselves. In this, the government should offer then as much help as possible instead of holding out the threat of a uniform system of mandatory numerical quota."

However, the major of the OBCs and other marginalized groups are mainly facing the problem of the lack of access to quality school education. "Reservations in jobs or higher education tackles the problem at the higher end. It needs to be supplemented by measures to improve the quality of teaching in government schools. This is where the real focus of governmental policy should be." For democratic solidarity, it is imperative to obliterate caste difference and encourage social harmony without any difference based on caste. It is the duty of the state to treat all its citizens equally as is the duty of modify the social and governmental structures to accommodate the legitimate demands of its minorities, which should be done rationally.

Despite socio-economic backwardness, it is also observed that, there are enough qualified people among Dalits in various fields who are competent to shoulder any job even the difficult ones. It would be an interesting instance to quote that a leading industrial firm from Maharashtra even though its top officials belonged to a particular sub-caste of Brahmins, the industrial house was generous enough to send a dalit to London to acquire advanced learning in the leather industry.

Another arguments put forth in favour of reservations is that reservations just not mean accepting any one just on the criteria of birth. It simply means that a person having requisite qualification for a particular job should not be denied it, just because he is born in a particular caste. Noted economist Jayati Ghosh says that she has "no problems with OBC job quotas." She believes that social discrimination starts very early at the academic level in educational institutions. She observes another important phenomena in the corporate sector and in this regards, comments," The best jobs, and even the regular one, are almost inevitably filled by upper caste candidates. Ghosh believes that even though talent and intelligence are widely and equally distributed among all classes of people, when it comes to education and jobs, the reserved classes take a backseat." She considers reservations as transparent and easy-to-monitor form and affirmative action and presents two arguments in favour of reservations, firstly, that merit is not concentrated in the upper classes and secondly, that development must always be a socially inclusive process."

A lasting solution to the problems of backward castes would be to provide economic empowerment and social emancipation. Economic empowerment as a concept means little as it does not provide a homogenous identification as can be made of social and cultural terms. Upward mobility of a group, collectively in totality, makes little sense when economic empowerment is considered as the prime mover.

Reservations in jobs, if at all a means for social and individual emancipation, must give way to new innovation. New ways must be found to reach the goal of emancipation without creating disenchantment with others. For the upliftment of communities and individuals, we have to go beyond the prism of reservations in the corporate sector.

Priority should be given to areas that are crucial, such as development of infrastructure and compulsory free education for the underprivileged. It is a widespread belief that primary and secondary education system has failed to deliver. There should be vocational opportunities for the employment and employment oriented skill to the backward castes. By attending to these basic necessities, marginalized groups will be empowered to complete fairly with those who are already privileged. Mere reservations of jobs will not help.

The widening gap between the private and public sector is clearly visible. The performance of private sector has been much better than the public, should be a good enough reason to rescruitinize the reservation of jobs. It needs to be seen if the failure results from flaws in the conception of the policy or in its implementation so, instead of proposing reservations in the private sector, government should think of alternative frameworks for social and economic upliftment.

Instead of demanding the "standard reservation format," they should aspire for better training and education standards which is going to serve as the most trusted guarantor for success. By giving people from the economically unprivileged classes incentives to develop can be a solution. This would not only be instrumental in filling the reservations posts that are lying vacant for the want of qualified backward classes candidates, but would also open up more avenues for the members of these communities in their drive to live better and more fulfilling lives.

CHAPTER 11

Disability and Reservations in India

There is no universally agreed definition of disability. Disability can be seen basically as a medical condition—'a problem located within the individual. Disability, is also reconcepualised primarily as a social phenomena. The social model of disability distinguishes between 'impairments' and 'disability'. 'It is society that disables people who have impairments, by failing to recognise and accommodate difference, and through the attitudinal, environmental and institutional barriers that it erects against people with impairment. "Disability, in the way, arises from a complex inter action between "health conditions and the context in which they exist. "In this way it is apply said, "your frame of mind is the real disability."

It is not tragic to be on the wheel chair rather it is more tragic when society when society fails to provide the things one needs to lead one's life in that condition. Disabled suffer from discriminatory treatment in the society and suffer from social exclusion.

DFID's working definition of social exclusion is:

" ... the experience of certain groups who suffer

discrimination on the basis of their social identity and are excluded from economic, social or political opportunities as a result. This discrimination may operate at the level of state policy, institutional bias, social practices, or historic neglect."

Chambers 2005

Disabled people are often, excluded from social and religion activities. They face severe barriers and thus, are excluded from educational, economic and cultural spheres and development, as well.

Here are few forms of disability, that are very common in the community, which we are aware of:

(1) Health Disabilities

- Amputation
- Spine bijida
- Degerecative disabilities
- Parkinson's discase
- Osteoporosis
- Arthritis
- Uzheimer's Disease
- Demertia
- Multiple Sclerosis
- Paralysis and special cold injury
- Polio
- Leprosy
- Stroke

(2) Learning Disabilities

- ADD (Attention Deficit Disorder)
- Autism
- Dyslexia

(3) Meaning and Visual Disabilities

- Deafness
- Visual Impairment
- Hearing Impairment
- Blindness

The world for and of the disabled is changing at a rapid pace. Many factors instrumental in these are advances in medical and surgical sciences, breakthroughs in technology, greater understanding of the causes of disability, improved method of coping with it, increasing consciousness of the civil rights. The human rights movements have vigorously expounded the cause of disabled to protect their basic right to dignity and self-respect.

In the present scenario, disabled are viewed as individuals with a wide range of abilities and each one of them willing and capable to utilize his/her potential and talents. While, society is considered the real cause of the misery of people with disabilities since it puts numerous barriers as expressed in education, employment, architecture, transport, health and other activities.

This social understanding of disability is accepted largely, and is reflected in the UN World Programme of Action for Disabled Persons, the Standard Rules on the Equalization of opportunities for persons with Disabilities, the World Health Organization's International Classification of Functioning Disability and Health (ICF) and by the World Bank, etc.

DISABILITY IN INDIA

Disability was included in the census for the first time in 2001, following a sustained campaign by the Indian disability movement. The census found that 2.2 per cent of the population were disabled. However, this figure is contested by organisations working in the field, which estimate India's total disabled population at approximately six per cent or 70 million —a figure larger than the entire population of the United Kingdom.

Disability Data for India

Total disabled	*Male*	*Female*	*Urban*	*Rural*
21,906,769	12,605,635	9,301	5,518,387	16,388,382

Source: Government of India (2001).

Disability Data for DFID Target States

	Andhra Pradesh	*Madhya Pradesh*	*Orissa*	*West Bengal*
Total disabled	1,364,981	1,408,528	1,021,335	1,847,174
In seeing	581,587	636,214	514,104	862,073
In speech	138,974	75,825	68,673	170,022
In hearing	73,373	85,354	84,115	131,579
In movement	415,848	495,878	250,851	412,658
Mental	155,199	115,257	103,592	270,842

Source: Government of India (2001).

Poverty is the biggest cause of disability in India. Also, various other factors like low literary and employment rates and wide-spread social stigma leave the physically challenged behind. The 360 million Indian people who live below the poverty line are most vulnerable to disability. This is because they are more likely to:

- suffer from malnutrition
- live in crowded and unsanitary conditions, making them more at risk of catching infectious diseases
- have limited access to medical care
- consult traditional healers
- be poorly educated and lack basic knowledge
- not immunize their children
- lack proper care during pregnancy and birth, and have multiple pregnancies.

In a large country like India, with a large number of disabled people who face various impediments to their growth like scarce resources and unhealthy social attitude like in education, employment, public services, means of transport, communication, etc. The dominant attitude towards disability is one of social welfare and disabled people are seen as passive victims requiring charitable help rather than equal citizens with potential. This remains in conformity with the broader understanding of rights in the country. In India, rights are not visualized on equality of access but rest on the notion that certain groups are underprivileged and require 'special' assistance.

In this the role of the state is important, whose role is to recognise and enshrine the rights of disabled people, and define responsibilities in legislation and policy. This can take the form of specific legislation and policy, or a comprehensive review of existing legislative and policy commitments, to ensure that the rights of disabled people are adequately protected and discrimination is removed.

It is a general understanding that legislation can bring respite to them and change the fabric of society for their betterment. There has been an increasing awareness in countries opting for laws favourable to disabled people. These legislation establishes a coherent and comprehensive framework for the promotion of just and fair policies and their effective implementation, which in the long run, will prove instrumental in full and total integration of the disabled in the society.

The Indian disability law treats disability, as a civil rights rather than a health and welfare issue. The Law recognizes that the primary issue facing disabled people is their exclusion from the mainstream activities of the society and hence the emphasis in the Law is on full integration and participation. It is discrimination, and not impairment, that disables people. The Law recognizes the importance of consultation with disabled people on issues which directly or indirectly affect them. The government, therefore, has set up mechanisms for consultations with people with all types of disabilities. Thus, those measures are carefully avoided which remove one group's barriers but increase them for addition to the statutory provisions and the services rendered by NGOs, a tremendous amount of informal support is given by the families and friends of the disabled. There are still many voluntary agencies and private enterprises with immense potential to contribute to the creation of a just and caring society in India. Without disabled people's rights being clearly entrenched in the law, there could be no progress in changing age old attitudes and improving the quality of life for people with disabilities.

The legislative framework for the protection of the rights of disabled people are mentioned in the following four acts:

- Mental Health Act, 1987
- Rehabilitation Council of India Act, 1992
- Persons with Disabilities (Equal Opportunities, Protection of Rights, and Full Participation) Act, 1995
- The National Trust Act for Welfare of Persons with Autism, Cerebral Palsy, Mental Retardation and Multiple Disability Act, 1999

These are outlined below:

Mental Health Act, 1987

This Act replaced the Indian Lunacy Act of 1912 and aims to introduce changes based on modern understanding of mental health and consolidate treatment and care practices in line with modern practices and values. Outmoded language was replaced, admission and discharge procedures simplified and psychiatric hospitals have to be licensed. The Act removed mental retardation from the definition of mental illness.

The Rehabilitation Council of India Act, 1992

This Act relates to the training of professionals in sixteen disciplines within the rehabilitation sector. It seeks to ensure that disabled people are treated by qualified personnel, and acts as an accreditation and quality control facility. The Act requires everyone practicing rehabilitation to register with the RCI's central rehabilitation register, but this is only possible with a government-recognised diploma. Following NGO lobbying, the Act has been diluted so that locally trained NGO personnel can be accredited after attending short courses at a range of government-approved training centres.

The Persons with Disabilities Act, 1995

The Indian Parliament, for the first time, has legally endorsed the right of access for the disabled people to education and vocational training; employment practices; travel on public transport and mobility schemes; barrier - free environment and integrated living; information and communication strategies; independence and dignity. The Persons with Disabilities (Equal Opportunities, Protection of Rights and Full Participation) Bill, 1995 was passed in December 1995 and was published in the Gazette of India on Monday, 1st January, 1996 after receiving consent from the President of India, Dr. Shankar Dayal Sharma. It became functional on 7th February, 1996.

The Persons with Disabilities (Equal Opportunities, Protection of Rights and Full Participation) Act, 1995 defines disability as one or more of the following: blindness, low vision, leprosy cured, hearing impairment, locomotor disability, mental retardation and mental illness. It says that to be considered disabled, a person must suffer from not less than 40 per cent of any disability as certified by a medical authority. The medical understanding of disability clearly informs the act, but its tight and selective definitions of disability, and its 40 per cent threshold, means that some key disabilities, such as autism and other spectrum disorders, haemophilia, thalassaemia, severe facial disfigurement, and individuals with more mild disabilities, are excluded.

This is the central government piece of legislation. The main provisions include:

- Prevention and early detection (section 25)
- Free education for every child with a disability in an appropriate environment until the age of 18 (section 26a)

- Schemes and programmes for non-formal education (section 27)
- A three per cent reservation admission to all government education institutions (section 39)
- A three per cent reservation in all government poverty alleviation schemes (section 40)
- Barrier-free environments in transport and government buildings (sections 44-46)
- A three per cent reservation in government posts and identification of posts for disabled people (sections 32a and 33)
- Special measures to overcome discrimination, such as preference in allotment of land for housing, business, special schools, research and recreation centres, and factories (section 43)
- Generic and specialised rehabilitation services (section 66)
- Insurance scheme for disabled employees (section 67)
- Unemployment allowance for out-of-work disabled people (section 68)
- Coordination and monitoring (chapters 2 and 3, section 3-24)
- Appointment of a commissioner in every state to follow up complaints (section 62).

To access the benefits of the Act, a disabled person must have a 'disability certificate', which is obtained after an assessment by certified government medical personnel. The assessment must find that the individual has a 40 per cent or above disability in visual impairment, hearing impairment, locomotor disability, cerebral palsy, leprosy cured, mental retardation, or mental illness.

So, the 1995, Disability Act provides three per cent reservations for disabled people in poverty alleviation programmes, government posts, and in state educational facilities, as well as other rights and entitlements.

One out of every ten people in India suffers from one form of disability or the other, that is they possess physical or mental impairment substantially limiting one or more of major life activities. In other words, 90 million of our countrymen live with, and learn to overcome in their own individual ways, problems which non-disabled can seldom understand. The, Disability law should enable not only one in ten people but nine out of every ten people to lead their lives to their fullest potential. The law declares that disability need not be insurmountable as long as it can be properly understood and catered for. The law attempts to eradicate factors which produce low self-esteem in disabled people and empowers them to confront the insensitivity and ignorance of others. The real danger now is that those who had been vigorously demanding its enactment might become complacent and think that the job has been done. The Act must be implemented in schools and colleges, in factories and workplaces, in transport and shopping Centres. People with disabilities, and those who care for them, must ensure that discrimination is outlawed and barriers are removed as much from the physical environment as from the attitudes of ordinary people. The real battle for the right to full citizenship and active participation of disabled people is ahead. The Act is comprehensive but must be enforced with sincerity and determination.

The National Trust Act, 1999

This Act aims to protect people with the seven impairments excluded under the 1995 Persons with Disability Act. It recognises that there are disabled people who will require care throughout their lives, and enables parents, relatives and organisations to request the appointment of a guardian for severely disabled people. The Act also provides for the bequest of property by parents of disabled children for future protection of their children after death.

ATTEMPTS OF MAINSTREAMING EDUCATION OF DISABLED STUDENTS IN INDIA

In the educational sector, the People with Disabilities have fared in a worse manner. If the very backward social categories, like SC, ST or Muslims have an out-of-school rate (the proportion of children who aren't in school) of 6-10% for the disabled it is as high as almost 38%. Newly one-third of children with mild disability are out of school, despite the fact that they needed no aids or appliances to be able to attend school. Yet, in respective of the levels of disability mild, moderate or severe—the disabled rarely progress beyond primary school. The out of school rate its more than fine and a half times the rate for all children which is less than 7%. Female illiteracy among the disabled is 64% and male illiteracy is 43%.

However, in India, the emphasis is not getting disabled children into school and providing assertive aids and improving the physical accessibility of school with the construction of ramps and rails.

Alongwith the promotion of integrated and inclusive education, there has been a rapid growth in the number of special schools. In the early 1990s, there were approximately 1,035 special schools, but by 2000 the number had more than doubled to reach around 2,500, with most concentrated in urban areas—particularly in Mumbai.

Disabled children who do manage to receive a basic education will encounter significant obstacles if they wish to further their studies. Despite the three per cent reservation in all state educational facilities, only 0.1 per cent of university students are disabled. Most universities are unaware of the assistance they can receive from the University Grants Commission (UGC) to improve accessibility. In a recent survey by NCPEDP, only nine per cent of the universities contacted had received a UGC grant. The situation is only slightly better at college level, where 0.52 per cent of the students were disabled.

However, in order to ensure that the education of disabled children be given equal importance, it is imperative that the "education is not treated as a welfare issue," but a right of all Indian citizen, including those with disabilities. Disabled children should have access to quality education. The Nationa Education Policy needs to reviewed. A clear stand of the nation regarding the education of disabled children, with due consideration to nation of impairment, severity of impairment, level of education, age etc. needs to be included in the policy. All other agencies which have the aim to impart education, like curriculum development, teachers' training, funding, etc., need to include disability in all their future agendas. The UGC needs to review the implementation of its schemes and take further proactive steps to enhance the access of higher education for disabled students.

Even though disabled people constitute a significant 5 to 6 percent of the population of India, their needs for meaningful employment remain unmet, inspite of the implementation of the 'The People with Disabilities' Act three years ago, which reserves 3 per cent in all categories of jobs in the government sector for disabled persons out of the approximately 70 million people with disabilities in India, only about 0.1 million have succeeded in getting employment in the industries till now.

The employment rate of physically challenged people is among the most excluded in the Indian job market, declined from 43 per cent in 1991 to 38 per cent in 2002 even in the midst of an economic reforms, a World Bank study said.

Many public sector companies do not employ disabled persons, even though it is legally binding on them to fill 3 per cent in all categories of jobs with disabled people. In the decade 1990's, employment of People with Disability (PWD) among large private firms was only 0.3 per cent of their workforce. Among the multinationals firms, the situation was far worse, with only 0.05 per cent being PWD. The industry, requires to play a more emphatic role because of their vast employment generating potential and the financial power.

So, even after three years of implementing the policy of job reservation for the disabled persons through a law, the targets achieved present a dismal picture. Even this level of achievement is only fulfilled through the employment of people with a relatively mild degree of disability. Inspite of various measures taken by the government there are limiting factors that prevent employment of disabled persons in the industry, education and employment.

Education is the key to the advancement of persons with disabilities as it provides access to information, enables them to communicate their needs, interests and experiences and bring them into contact of other people, enthusing them with the spirit to assert their rights. Without the basic education, the chances of employment become rare. Hence, the policies and programmes that will place disabled people in the mainstream education system, remains by and large an important objective of the government.

So, there is an urgent need to identify the factors that widen their employment potential of disabled people and also to take corrective measures to enlarge the political measures of their rehabilitation and social integration.

However, there are enormous barriers in the path of disabled children in getting equal access to education in India. The position, in India, in the field of education remains absolutely critical to enable disabled children to realise their abilities, and the government acknowledges that the vast majority have no access to education at all. The office of the Chief Commission for Persons with Disabilities estimates that not more than four per cent of disabled children are receiving formal education, while the Ministry of Human Resource Development (MHRD) and National Council of Education Research and Training (NCERT) puts the figure at less than one per cent.

FUTURE DIRECTIONS

Today, the emphasis is on inclusive education which aims at systemic transformation and makes it a key strategy for achieving education for all and improving the quality of education. It is a process control on transforming the teaching styles and learning environment to meet the special educational needs of children, rather than making the child adjust to an existing system.

CHAPTER 12

Equity Vs. Equality

THE HIGHEST EQUALITY IS EQUITY
VICTOR HUGO

We often say that people should be treated equally, while what we mean is that they should be treated fairly and being 'equal' does not necessarily translate to being fair. After all, one wouldn't expect two people of different capabilities to perform the same task identically. Say you buy a book on advanced philosophy—you might understand what you are reading, but an average high school student probably wouldn't. Similarly, the average forty-year-old swimmer probably wouldn't be able to swim twenty laps of the pool in the same time as a twenty year old. A teacher might need to spend a lot more time explaining a concept to an average student than he would to a brilliant one. If he spent equal time with both, then neither would benefit—the former might not understand, while the latter would probably be bored. Thus, to ensure that both students perform well and gain from the exercise, the teacher would treat them equitably, according to their different requirements, rather than equally.

Thus, though equality and equity sound similar, they are actually quite different.

Equality implies sameness. Ideally, it would manifest in our world through equal starting points (as in equal opportunities for everyone, which is practically impossible given the diversity of social and economic backgrounds); or in equal access for all to resources (again, this is unlikely without a high degree of societal affluence and philanthropy); or in equal outcomes (also unachievable given the prevailing forms of inequality). Thus, the term equality can only be used in the formal sense to mean every individual's status as a human being who has 'equal rights' to leverage his or her own abilities, talents, etc. to the extent of their own ambition and within the confines of the law and societal mores.

Equality is, however, a useful formal yardstick against which to estimate the more meaningful concept of equity: the notion of fairness and justice and empowerment, of everyone getting a fair deal in the real sense. People who are treated equitably are treated fairly-which may not be equally.

EQUITY IS EQUALITY LACED WITH WISDOM AND JUDGMENT

When people are treated equally, differences are ignored. When they are treated equitably, differences are recognized, and also used properly to realize each person's potential to the fullest extent possible.

The essential difference between equality and equity is that equity starts with an assumption of difference, of separate starting points, an acknowledgement that people have diverse experiences, values, and abilities. It respects that difference. Despite race, gender, and social differences coming in the way, the concept of equity is more realistic starting point for achieving equal outcomes than equality.

THE IDEAL OF EQUALITY IN AMERICA AND INDIA

Equality is often considered the fundamental American value, the sacred value of the country. Political equality has been part of the American mythology ever since the founders of the country created the Constitution—"We hold these truths to be self-evident, that all men are created equal..."

Noted author and Nobel Peace Prize winner Elie Weisel, when asked what the American Dream meant to him, said: "Equality in diversity. That no group should be superior in the American society than another."

Nature is unimaginably diverse and two people are the same. In the entire animate world, there is nothing distantly resembling equality. In fact, there is only diversity to be seen, and this is most obvious in humans. Each individual, despite certain apparent similarities, differs from others in countless ways with unique physical, mental, emotional, and behavioral makeup. No person can ever be equal to another; so the assertion that "all men are created equal" is simply not true. Dr. Ludwig Von Mises said "the fact that men are born unequal in regard to physical and mental capacities cannot be argued away. Some surpass their fellow men in health and vigor, in brains and aptitudes, in energy and resolution and are, therefore, better fitted for the pursuit of earthly affairs than the rest of mankind." Thus, complete equality is unnatural, impossible to achieve, essentially an impossible state. While no one is equal by nature, all should have the freedom to exploit their capabilities without regard to race, religion, disability, and gender. This, while not yet fully realized, is a desired natural state.

The diversity and inequality of human beings forms the basis of much of our civilized social order. If all individuals were the same, there would be no division of labour, no trade, and probably no social intercourse. It is the differences between individuals, not their similarities, which provide us with opportunity for growth and for an ever evolving and richer society. Diversity enables division of labour, makes trade possible, and is the very bedrock of our survival in a myriad ways.

Even when the difficulties and the impossibility of social equality are obvious, the proponents of equality demand, not equality per se, but "equality of opportunity." Most often this is defined in a very loose fashion as a sense of fair play necessary in playing the "game of life." There have been large strides made towards equality in the US—but attention should now be focused toward equity, which is a more achievable state.

Friedrick Hayek, one of the twentieth century's leading capitalist economists and winner of the Nobel Prize, once said, "From the fact that people are very different it follows that, if we treat them equally, the result must be inequality in their actual position, and that the only way to place them in an equal position would be to treat them differently. Equality before the law and material equality are therefore not only different but are in conflict which each other; and we can achieve either one or the other, but not both at the same time."

The Indian society has been based on the idea of equality of opportunity for each individual rather than equality of results. This has, if anything, grown stronger over time. Although a reasonably progressive taxation system and a network of redistributive social programs serve to smooth extreme disparities, these interventions generally play a smaller role than in most other industrialized nations. There is an emphasis on establishing a fair process to guide the initial competition rather than on altering the distribution of rewards. The governmental efforts in our country have been directed towards creating a "level playing field," on which all individuals have equal opportunity regardless of race, sex, caste or religion; and equipping individuals with the tools necessary for success by widening access to education.

Historically, the ideal of equal opportunity in the Indian State has been so grossly compromised by differential treatment of particular groups that much of the nation's political energy has been engaged by efforts to put right these injustices.

Since individuals vary so much, equality of opportunity is simply not feasible. What equality of opportunity can there be, for example, between two people, one extremely intelligent but sickly, and the other in perfect health but not particularly clever? Is it not obvious that they will have different roles in life, that no amount of equal opportunity will enable to achieve the same outcomes, and that what they need is unequal opportunities in accord with their unequal aptitudes? Just as no equality of endowment of the human beings is possible, nor can be there a truly equal environment.

Equal Employment Opportunity (EEO) is a term used by the government to refer to employment practices that ensure nondiscrimination on the basis of race, sex, religion, color, national origin, physical or mental ability, medical condition, ancestry, or age. In other words, everyone should have the same access to opportunities. Reservation is one aspect of the government's efforts to ensure employment opportunities to all, its purpose being to promote fairness and address the effects of past discrimination in employment by encouraging targeted outreach efforts to attract the minorities and women.

The political system in India and the United States has enacted numerous policies to ensure the equality promised to all the people of the nation. Policy makers fight every day about a person's ability to receive the same equal opportunities and equal results (or outcomes) as everyone else. The difference between equal opportunity and equal outcomes, however, must be clearly distinguished. An employer who offers equal opportunity does not discriminate on the basis of a person's race, creed, or disability, and so makes sure that everyone has a chance to achieve a certain outcome. Equal outcomes means making sure that everyone gets the same place. Equal outcome can be considered discriminatory because it looks at a person's race, creed, or disability in order to place them where they can finish the race at the same time. Each of these policies has benefited society. Equal Opportunity Employment has made it possible for people of all castes and religions to enter the national workforce, and so diversified the workplace. Equal Outcome policies have made strides to ensure that all races, religions, creeds, and people with disabilities are proportionally represented in the workplace, giving minorities the motivation to strive for the best and eventually eliminate the need for an equal outcome policy.

However, equal opportunity policies that focus more on equal outcome policies such as quotas can be unfair, because a better qualified person may be passed over in favor of the minority required to fill a certain quota. Employers may focus on the quotas, hence diminishing the value diversity offers in and of itself.

The benefits of working in a multicultural, diverse work environment are many. In the globalized, modern and evolving workplace, there are countless opportunities to learn about other cultures. Like America is a huge melting pot of cultures and people from all walks of life who need to co-exist and learn from each other because they are different, India, a land of diversities, if represented in a balanced way can be a rich heritage and asset to the world. This learning can help us become more positive, understanding, tolerant, and efficient. The changing demographics of the workforce are an inevitable phenomenon. For the open-minded employee, the transition to a more diverse work environment can be an exciting and enriching new experience.

The Indian society has always been hierarchical in structure and heterogeneous in composition. It has been caste ridden and so never organized on the principles of equity. It was major objective of the Indian Constitution to restructure unequal Indian society on the principles of equity. India is constitutional democracy that underlines the idea of providing equity in social and political life and preserves civil liabilities, individual rights and equality of opportunity along with providing a separate 'social space' for its identities. The Indian democracy has taken various measures to address the needs of the backward sections of the society, to provide equality of opportunity to them and to put an end to discrimination against the people who have been subjected to discriminatory practices. Rajeev Bhargava says, "To tackle the basic inequalities already existing in the Indian social structure, and to make the formal political empowerment of severely disadvantaged groups more effective, the introduction of constitutionally protected preferential treatment of these groups was thought necessary. A mere right to vote and to equality of opportunity, it was widely recognized, is insufficient to ensure meaningful, effective social and political equality. Thus, apart from several general provisions to the right to equality, special constitutional measures were taken to protect and advance the interests of the Scheduled Castes and Scheduled Tribes."

The Constitution of India provided for Equality before law as well as Equalityof opportunity. So, the Article 16 of the Indian Constitution, while referring to Equality of opportunity in matters of public employment, also made a provision for reservations of the posts for "the backward class of citizens. The various features introducing protective discrimination are a distinct feature of the Constitution of India since 1950. The Constitution of India incorporates explicit provisions for reservations in favour of the backward groups namely the Scheduled Castes (SCs) and the Scheduled Tribes (STs) and also for other 'Weaker Sections' or 'Backward Classes'.

These and other measures aim to make the society inclusive, organize on the principles of equity and integrate the minorities into the mainstream. In order to achieve it, it was considered prerequisite to avail the constitutional safeguards which would grant an initial push to the people who have remained oppressed and marginalized for a long period of time due to caste-based excesses of the dominant sections of society. These measures will be instrumental in cultivating self-confidence in them and empower them to prove themselves in the conditions of open competition.

Hence, the concept of reservation can be used as a constructive tool of social engineering and moving towards a just society. We cannot treat two unequals equally for it would be unjust to do so, in the same way as we would treat two equals unequally. In a society like India that is highly unequalitarian, protective policies are instrumental in inclusive development of all the segments of society. It can accelerate the process of secularization and challenge the hegemony of the dominant castes. It would also create a fair chance of representation of the downtrodden segments in social institutions, state apparatuses and also, market. In the interest of social and distributive justice a liberal democracy like India the democratic procedures and institutions, the state has to work in a manner which facilitates the promotion of tolerance and cultural co-existence. The dilemma can be resolved only when the cultural, linguistic, regional, caste and religious difference are not considered antithetical to the spirit of national unity and there is no dichotomy between unity and diversity.

Equity is about a fair go for all. Diversity is about recognizing and embracing differences. Applied together they provide a holistic approach to management and leadership aimed at creating a work environment that uses and values the talents, abilities and contributions of all people.

APPENDIX

Moily Committee Report

INTRODUCTION

1.1. The **Oversight Committee** was constituted under the orders of the Prime Minister on the 27th May, 2006 to look, *inter alia*, into the following aspects and submit its report by the 31st August 2006 (subsequently extended to the 30th September, 2006).

(1) "Implementation of 27% reservation for the OBCs in Institutes of Higher Learning, and

(2) Assessment of additional infrastructure and other requirements for increasing the overall availability of seats to a level so that the present level of seats available to the general category students does not decline."

1.2. In addition, the PMO constituted five specialist groups to go into detail "about the course of action to be adopted for giving effect to the implementation of reservation in a time bound manner."

1.3. The Oversight Committee, under the chairmanship of **Shri M. Veerappa Moily**, held five preliminary meetings and separate discussions with the Heads of the Groups. A *Theme Paper* was prepared and placed on the website.

1.4. The Interim Report laid down certain principles based on which the Committee decided to carry out its mandate. These principles are being recounted below:

(a) The Oversight Committee would cover such

institutions of higher learning which have already implemented reservations for SCs/STs.

(b) Institutions primarily engaged in R&D will not fall within this ambit.

(c) The programme and guidelines drawn up by the Oversight Committee, with the help of the Groups, would act as a point of reference and help the other Ministries of the Government of India to take such measures to introduce reservations in institutions of higher learning from the academic year 2007-08.

(d) The moving spirit behind the new reservation policy will be **expansion, inclusion and excellence**. The Central Institutions will keep these three principles in view while determining threshold marks for admission of OBC students. Institutions like IITs, IISc, IIMs and AIIMS and other such exceptional quality institutions can only maintain their standards if they are given full autonomy in determining the threshold limits for admissions and in inducting top-class faculty.

(e) 'Cut-offs' for institutions other than the IITs, IIMs, IISc & AIIMS, may be placed somewhere midway between those for SC & ST and the unreserved category, carefully calibrated so that the principles of both *equity* and *excellence* can be maintained.

(f) While expanding the intake, due care should be taken to ensure that capacities are expanded in subjects or areas in which there are opportunities on account of employability.

(g) The students who currently tend to get excluded must be given every single opportunity to raise their own levels of attainment, so that they can reach their true potential. For this, Government must invest heavily in creating powerful, well-designed and executed remedial preparatory measures, to enable these students in overcoming their initial handicap. These guiding principles providing the bedrock of premises of action on which the Oversight Committee framed its recommendations in the Interim Report.

(h) In its first meeting, on the 30th May 2006, the Committee took note of the fact that the main problem lies in increasing the strength of the faculty, especially in institutions where there is already a backlog of vacancies. It was felt that while the 'core compensation' package of academic staff should not be altered to avoid disturbing the existing parities, there was a case for providing non-monetary incentives and, for institutions of excellence, the remuneration system should be made more flexible so as to attract talent and to make the faculty appointments more attractive.

1.5. It is essential to reproduce the relevant portions of the Interim Report laying down the recommendations relating to faculty and infrastructure issues in order to provide the background for the further deliberations of the Committee that have led to this Final Report:-

I. Recommendations on Academic and Faculty-related Issues

30. The Directors of the Institutes and Group Members expressed concern about the availability of suitable personnel for filling up of additional faculty positions, in such a short span of time. In many institutions and in many departments particularly in IITs and IIMs, it has not been possible to fill up even the existing vacancies. It was, therefore, the unanimous opinion of all groups that very innovative methods will have to be found for retaining or re-engaging the existing personnel, particularly those who have either superannuated during

recent years or those who are likely to superannuate during the next three years. This would be in addition to making optimal use of the existing faculty. The suggestions received in this regard have a wide range and need to be given serious consideration:-

(a) Raising the age of superannuation to 65 years (across the Board) and/or

(b) Engaging retiring faculty on a 3-years contract, extendable up to the age of 70 years. Renewal to be based on a review of performance by the Academic Boards.

Suggestion (b) should be operational for a minimum time period required to achieve a smooth transition to expanded intake, till the regular faculty gets into position.

31. The Oversight Committee considers expansion, inclusion and excellence as the moving spirit behind the new reservation policy. The institutions of higher learning should keep these three principles in view while determining threshold marks for admission to OBC students. While expanding the intake, due care should be taken to ensure that capacities are expanded in subjects or areas in which there are opportunities on account of employability.

32. The Committee recognizes that those institutions of higher learning which have established a global reputation (e.g. IITs, IIMs, IISc, AIIMS and other such exceptional quality institutions), can only maintain that if the highest quality in both faculty and students is ensured. Therefore, the committee recommends that the threshold for admission should be determined by the respective institutions alone, as is done today, commensurate with the level of its excellence.

33. As regards 'cut-offs' in institutions other than those mentioned in para 7, these may be placed somewhere midway between those for SC/ST and the unreserved category,

carefully calibrated so that the principles of both equity and excellence can be maintained.

34. The Committee strongly feels that the students who currently tend to get excluded, must be given every single opportunity to raise their own levels of attainment, so that they can reach their true potential. The Government should invest heavily in creating powerful, well designed and executed remedial preparatory measures to achieve this objective fully.

Other recommendations are:-

(a) Engaging visiting or adjunct faculty - on attractive terms;

(b) Assigning additional workload to existing faculty, within reasonable limits so that there is no dilution. For motivating the existing faculty additional compensation may be contemplated;

(c) Amendment in eligibility criteria for faculty recruitment. The requirement of a Ph.D. qualification could be considered for waiver by the concerned academic authority where a faculty member has enough relevant experience, like a practicing manager, for example. The Committee is aware that the UGC have made certain relaxations in respect of faculty qualifications.

(d) Autonomy may be given to the relevant Academic Bodies of each institution to undertake the special recruitment process in a speedy manner.

(e) Autonomy will also have to be given in respect of the compensation packages to be offered in contractual engagements. Here, providing residential facilities to faculty on contract or reemployed teachers is recommended so as to retain qualified teachers.

(f) The Committee would support the stand of the Engineering and Technology Group in their specific demands for a one time joining allowance/relocation grant, jobs for spouses and assured admission in schools to children so as to reduce attrition among competent faculty.

(g) The Committee shares that Group's proposal for developing an action plan for Quality Improvement and upgrading the skills of the existing faculty. The establishment if a National Centre for Faculty Development and also conducting sequential summer programmes for faculty development would provide affirmative action with long term benefits.

(h) The Teacher Student Ratio (TSR) varies from Group to Group and the Committee would like to categorically state that enhancement of faculty should be based on a rational and viable teacher student ratio. An unreasonable and nonviable teacher student ratio would impede the process of implementing the reservation policy.

(i) Suitable policy changes in enhancement of the retirement age, contractual appointments, modifications in eligibility conditions for faculty, lifting of the ban on recruitment of non-academic staff, provision for adequate support staff will have to be effected immediately so that the special recruitment process can be set in motion.

(j) The Medical Council of India (MCI) will have to expedite changes in their norms relating to teacher student ratio and other academic norms (relating to number of UG seats) to ensure implementation of OBC reservation from the coming academic year.

II. Recommendations on Infrastructural and Developmental Issues

35. In order to ensure that the additional student intake will be matched by commensurate infrastructural facilities, a plan for developmental expansion has been submitted by each

Group. Subsequently, each institution will prepare a detailed Project Report giving timelines and required budgetary outlays. It is suggested that the Committee makes the following recommendations relating to infrastructure:

1. In general, all institutions will need additional physical space, construction of new college and hostel buildings, additional laboratories, library facilities, books, furniture and equipment, computer laboratories, campus wireless connectivity, video conferencing and IT enabled classrooms. Optimal use should also be made of the existing infrastructure.
2. The other major elements of the capital cost would be relating to residential accommodation for teaching staff and in some special cases non-teaching staff.
3. The procedures involved in setting up additional infrastructure especially civil works and procurement of furniture and equipment, have laid down administrative procedures.
4. Necessary delegation of powers and increased autonomy will have to be provided so as to ensure that the necessary infrastructure will be put in position at the earliest.
5. The Committee recommends the setting up of an **Empowered Committee** in each institution and Ministry, which will give the necessary approvals and sanctions.
    - This Empowered Committee can be constituted in each institution as per their relevant governing norms. The Empowered Committee should be given clear cut terms of reference with appropriate powers of delegation.
    - The delegation must ensure that the local unit will have the powers to issue necessary administrative orders for undertaking civil works and procurement of furniture and equipment.

- The Empowered Committee will also supervise the implementation of the development plan, observance of timelines and quality aspects of the projects' execution.
- Suitable policies will have to be notified for establishment of the Empowered Committee and also for delegation of financial and administrative powers.

6. Each Group has broadly laid down the infrastructural requirements. However, the specific requirements institution-wise will also have to be taken into account, which would figure in the final report. The Groups should attempt preparation of institution-wise DPRs.
7. There will be an **Implementation Monitoring Committee** in the Planning Commission, which will review the progress in the implementation of the OBC reservation plan and the execution of DPRs.
8. Wherever land acquisition is necessary for setting up the infrastructure, appropriate administrative orders will have to be issued for removing any bottlenecks and for placing the process on a fast track.
9. In order to ensure that the process of expansion commences immediately, release of adequate proportionate funds will have to be effected. This is essential for timely implementation.
10. The additional infrastructure will involve sizable non-recurring capital costs and also recurring costs, which are being projected separately.
11. Each group will have to submit an institution-wise detailed project report drawing up the master plan for expansion.

36. The Oversight Committee is committed to its mandate that the implementation process needs to commence from

2007-08. However, certain issues and constraints have been posed by the institutions through the groups concerning the time frame for implementation, especially the possibility of sudden expansion leading to loss of merit and excellence. These issues and practical constraints will be addressed by the Oversight Committee, institution wise, on receipt of the Groups' Final Reports.

1.6 Although it was not required to do so, the **Oversight Committee** submitted its **Interim Report** to the Prime Minister on the 27th July in order to assess the dimensions of the issues involved and facilitate legislation proposed by the Ministry of Human Resource Development (MHRD), consequent to the notification of the Constitution (Ninety-Third Amendment) Act, 2005. The Notification brought into effect the 104th Amendment to the Constitution in January this year to provide, *inter alia*, reservations for students coming from the socially and educationally backward classes of citizens, popularly known as other backward classes **(OBCs)**. The Interim Report, the preliminary financial statements that were attached thereto and the Theme Paper.

1.7. Consequent to the submission of the Interim Report, the Oversight Committee decided to hold detailed discussions with each of the specialist groups where representatives of all the institutions of higher learning were invited to attend so that their viewpoint could be heard and understood. Meetings were accordingly held with the Group on the 17th, 18th, 21st and 22nd August, 2006. In order to obtain a broader perspective on some of the issues involved, the Committee invited experts from each discipline for discussions on the Groups' final reports on the 28th and 29th of August, 2006.

RESERVATION FOR OBCS (27%): A ROADMAP FOR IMPLEMENTATION

3.1 The implementation of the 27 per cent reservation of seats for OBCs in the Institutes of Higher Learning will begin from 2007-08. All discussions, deliberations, and consultations with respect to the time-frame of the implementation, show that there are several constraints and difficulties in the implementation of the 27 per cent quota at one go. But, it should be possible to fully implement the same within the span of a maximum of three years. However, there are also instances where some Institutes have shown willingness and capacity to implement the Reservation Policy within less than a three-year period. The Oversight Committee, therefore, recommends that all Institutes of Higher Learning should fully implement the quota within the maximum period of three years and all such Institutes which have capacity to implement within less than three-year period, say within one year or within two years, should do so without taking recourse to the three year time frame. Under no circumstances can the time-limit of three years for implementation be overstepped.

IMPLEMENTATION RELATED ISSUES

4.1 The discussions with the groups, experts and others brought out a number of related issues.

TREATMENT OF THE CREAMY LAYER:

4.1 One of the main residual issues mentioned in the *interim report* was the application of the ***creamy layer*** concept in respect of reservation for **OBCs**. This was discussed in some detail and the decision taken was to leave the matter to the Government of India, keeping in mind the fact that the 'creamy layer' is not covered in the Central Educational Institutions (Reservation in Admissions) Bill, 2006, which has been introduced in Parliament, and as some members felt that this subject was beyond the purview of this Committee. A short study made for the Oversight Committee in the Planning Commission indicates, *inter alia*, that:

(a) Since income is a major determinant of the ability to access higher education, it may be necessary to supplement reservations with a merit-cum-means scholarship programme, as is being done for SC/STs.

(b) The true benefit of reservations will be realized only when the high school enrolment of OBCs, especially in rural areas, increases significantly. Attention will need to be paid to this issue in the coming years.

1.1 One of the main related issues mentioned in the Interim Report was the application of the ***creamy layer*** concept in respect of reservation for OBCs. During the deliberations of the Oversight Committee, one view which was expressed was that the Committee must give its recommendations in respect of the "creamy layer" problem. The fact that the Government has not taken a decision in respect of applying the "creamy layer" should not preclude the Committee from giving a categorical recommendation in this regard. During the discussion, in the final meeting of the Committee, however, it was felt that this was beyond the mandate of the Committee.

1.2 It may be recalled that the issue of the 'creamy layer' was not examined in detail in the report of the Backward Classes Commission (popularly referred to as the ***Mandal Commission***) in 1980. The matter however, come up before the Supreme Court in Writ Petition (in Civil) No. 930 of 1990, delivered on the 16th November, 1992 (*Indira Sawhney & Others Vs. Union of India & others*). In the Judgment, though their Lordships made their observations separately, almost all of them were of the view that the socially and educationally, as well as economically advanced members of the OBCs should be excluded from the benefits of reservation in view of the fact that the basis for such reservation is ***class*** and not ***caste***.

1.3 The creamy layer persons/sections defined by the Expert Committee which were accepted and notified by the Government vide O.M. No. 36012/22/93-Estt. (SCT) dated 8-9-1993 are classified into the following categories:

CREAMY LAYER

Description of category	*To whom rule of exclusion will apply*
I. Constitutional Posts	Sons and daughter(s) of— (a) President of India; (b) Vice-President of India; (c) Judges of the Supreme Court and of the High Courts; (d) Chairman and Members of UPSC and of the State Public Service Commission; Chief Election Commission; Comptroller and Auditor-General of India; (e) Persons holding constitutional positions of like nature.
II. Service Category A Group 'A'/Class I Officers of the All India Central and State Services (Direct Recruits)	Son(s) and daughter(s) of — (a) parents, both of whom are Class I officers; (b) parents, either of whom is a Class I officer; (c) parents, both of whom are Class I officers, but one of them dies or suffers permanent incapacitation; (d) parents, either of whom is a Class I officer and such parents dies or suffers permanent incapacitation and before such death or such incapacitation has had the benefit of employment in any International Organisation like UN, IMF, World bank, etc., for a period of not less than 5 years;

(Contd.)

Contd. ...

Description of category	*To whom rule of exclusion will apply*
	(e) parents, both of whom are Class I officers die or suffer permanent incapacitation and before such death or such incapacitation of the both either of them has had the benefit of employment in any International Organisation like UN, IMF, World Bank, etc. for a period of not less than 5 years; Provided that the rules of exclusion shall not apply in the following cases: (a) Sons and daughters of parents either of whom or both of whom are Class I officers and such parent(s) dies/die or suffer permanent incapacitation; (b) A lady belonging to OBC category has got married to a Class I officer, and may herself like to apply for job.
B. Group 'B'/Class II Officers of the Central and State Services (Direct Recruitment)	Son(s) and daughter(s) of - (a) parents, both of whom are Class II officers; (b) parents of whom only the husband is a Class II officer and he gets into Class I at the age of 40 or earlier; (c) parents, both of whom are Class II officers and one of them dies or suffers permanent incapacitation and either one of them has had the benefit of employment in any International Organisation UN, IMF, World Bank, etc., for a period of not less than 5 years before such death or permanent incapacitation;

	(d) parents of whom the husband is a Class I officer (direct recruitment or pre-forty promoted) and the wife is a Class II officer and the wife dies; or suffers permanent incapacitation; and (e) Parents, of whom the wife is a Class I officer (Direct Recruit or pre-forty promoted) and the husband is a Class II officer and the husband dies or suffers permanent incapacitation; Provided that the rule of exclusion shall not apply in the following cases:— Sons and daughters of — (a) Parents both of whom are Class II officers and one of them dies or suffers permanent incapacitation. (b) Parents, both of whom are Class II officers and both of them die or suffer permanent incapacitation, even though either of them has had the benefit of employment in any International Organisation like UN, IMF, World Bank, etc. for a period of not less than 5 years before their death or permanent incapacitation.
C. Employees in Public Sector Undertakings, etc.	The criteria enumerated in A and B above in this category will apply mutates mutandis to officers holding equivalent or comparable posts in PSUs, Banks, Insurance Organisations, Universities, etc., and also to equivalent or comparable posts and positions under private employment, pending the evaluation of the posts on equivalent or comparable basis in these institutions, the criteria specified in Category VI below will apply to the officers in these Institutions.

(Contd.)

Contd. ...

Description of category	*To whom rule of exclusion will apply*
III. Armed forces including Paramilitary Forces (Persons holding civil posts are not included)	Son(s) and daughter(s) of parents either or both of whom is or are in the rank of Colonel and above in the Army and to equivalent posts in the Navy and the Air Force and the Paramilitary Forces; Provided that - (i) If the wife of an armed forces officer is herself in the armed forces (i.e., the category under consideration) the rule of exclusion will apply only when she herself has reached the rank of Colonel; (ii) the service ranks below Colonel of husband and wife shall not be clubbed together; (iii) if the wife of an officer in the armed forces is in civil employment, this will not be taken into account for applying the rule of exclusion unless she falls in the service category under item No. II in which case the criteria and conditions enumerated therein will apply to her independently.
IV. Professional class and those engaged in Trade and Industry (i) Persons engaged in profession as a doctor, lawyer, chartered accountant, income tax consultant, financial or management consultant, dental	

surgeon, engineer, architect, computer specialist, film artists and other film professional, author, playwright, sports person, sports professional, media professional or any other vocations of like status.	
(ii) Persons engaged in trade, business and industry.	**Criteria specified against Category VI will apply** Criteria specified against Category VI will apply. Explanation— (i) Where the husband is in some profession and the wife is in a Class II or lower grade employment, the income/wealth test will apply only on the basis of the husband's income. (ii) If the wife is in any profession and the husband is in employment in Class II or lower rank post, then the income/wealth criterion will apply only on the basis of the wife's income and the husband's income will not be clubbed with it.
	V. Property Owners A. Agricultural holding. Son(s) and daughter(s) of persons belonging to a family (after, mother and minor children) which owns- (a) only irrigated land which is equal to or more than 85% of the statutory ceiling area, or

(Contd.)

Contd. ...

Description of category	*To whom rule of exclusion will apply*
	(b) both irrigated and unirrigated land, as follows: (i) The rule of exclusion will apply where the pre-condition exists that the irrigated area (having been brought to a single type under a common denominator) 40% or more of the statutory ceiling limit for irrigated land (this being calculated by excluding the unirrigated portion). If this pre-condition of not less than 40% exists, then only the area of unirrigated land will be taken into account. This will be done by converting, the unirrigated land on the basis of the conversion formula existing, into the irrigated type. The irrigated area so computed from unirrigated land and if after such clubbing together the total area in terms of irrigated land is 85% or more of the statutory ceiling limit for irrigated land, then the rule of exclusion will apply and disentitlement will occur.) (ii) The rule of exclusion will not apply if the land holding of a family is exclusively unirrigated.
B. Plantations (i) Coffee, tea, rubber, etc.	Criteria of income/wealth specified in Category VI below will apply.
(ii) Mango, citrus, apple plantations, etc.	Deemed as agricultural holding and hence criteria at A above under this category will apply Criteria specified in Category VI below will apply.

C. Vacant land and/or buildings in urban Agglomerations.	EXPLANATION: Building may be used for residential, industrial or commercial purpose and the like two or more such purposes.
VI. Income/Wealth Test	Son(s) daughter(s)— **(a) Persons having gross annual income of Rs. 1 lakh or above or possessing wealth above the exemption limit as prescribed in the Wealth Act for a period of three consecutive years (b) Persons in Categories I, II, III and VA who are not disentitled to the benefit of reservation but have income from other sources of wealth which will bring them within the income/wealth criteria mentioned in (a) above. EXPLANATION: (i) Income from salaries or agricultural land shall not be clubbed; (ii) The income criteria in terms of rupee will be modified taking into account the change in its value every three years. If the situation, however, so demands, the interregnum may be less. EXPLANATION—Whether the expression "permanent incapacitation" occur in this schedule, it shall mean incapacitation which results in putting an officer out of service.

Note: ** The Income limit has since been raised from Rs. 1 lakh to Rs. 2.5 lakh w.e.f. 09.03.2004 vide DOP2T O.M. No. 36033/3/2004-ESTT (Res) dated 09-03-2004.

Source: National Commission for Backward Classes website.

1.4 The principles upheld in *Indra Sawhney* have been maintained by the Supreme Court and reiterated in *JT 1999 (9) SC 557* delivered on 13/12/1999. *Indra Sawhney* clearly lays down that the creamy layer concept will not be applicable to the Scheduled Castes and Scheduled Tribes, and any misapprehensions on this account would be unfounded. In fact, Prime Minister Rajiv Gandhi also vehemently propounded the theory of excluding the creamy layer as he was apprehensive of the disadvantaged classes losing the benefits of reservation and upper layer of OBCs who are well of and have enjoyed the benefits for two or three generations continuing to be protected at the cost of the voiceless and deprived classes of OBCs for whom the process of empowerment is really meant.

1.5. The matter of applying the creamy layer concept in respect of reservations for students belonging to the OBCs in institutions of higher learning was discussed in the Committee. The Committee considered the argument that the idea of allowing the *creamy layer* the benefit of reservation would work against the interests of the poorer members of the OBCs and thereby defeat the underlying purpose of making higher education inclusive and equity based.

1.6. The status of the socio-economic development of OBCs in respect of such parameters as relate to poverty, health, education, unemployment, workforce participation, land ownership etc. The analysis of NSS data clearly brings out that inclusion of the *creamy layer* will result in reserved seats getting pre-empted by the OBCs from the top two income deciles at the cost of the poorer income deciles of the OBCs. *Thus almost all rural OBCs as well as Urban OBCs from the Northern, Central and Eastern regions of India will be deprived of the intended benefit of reservation.*

1.7. On the other hand, it was argued that if the *creamy layer* of OBCs is denied access to reservation in education *pari-passu* with the principle applied in the case of employment, the reserved for the OBCs. In a case study from Karnataka (included in Annexure X), it has been clearly shown that the OBC quotas have been utilized without any compromise with academic excellence in a situation where the creamy layer has been excluded. The apprehension that seats will not be filled up if the creamy layer is excluded has been comprehensively shown to be unfounded. The case study shows that the performance of students from below the creamy layer is outstanding and much better than general category students.

1.8. Nevertheless, to allay the fear of reserved seats remaining vacant, as a *vis-media*, an alternative formulation was submitted to the Committee which suggested that the creamy layer should be excluded in the first instance and a provision should be made that, keeping in view the prescribed threshold of qualifying marks, if after admitting non-creamy layer OBC candidates some reserve quota seats remain vacant, access could then be given to the *creamy layer* candidates in order of merit, after others are considered. This in fact amounts to giving non-creamy layer OBCs a right of way over the creamy layer OBCs.

1.9. Having considered the pros & cons and the *via-media*, it was, however, felt that the Oversight committee should leave it to the Government of India to take a decision regarding the applicability of the *creamy layer* concept and the alternative proposed could be considered.

1.10. At the last meeting of the Committee held on 27th September, 2006, a view was expressed that even a reference to the creamy layer would not be appropriate, keeping in view the limited mandate of the Committee. It was also claimed that the short study made on the status of *OBCs* was based on inadequate data, while some of the other members felt that the creamy layer concept should not be covered as the Central Educational Institutions (Reservation in Admissions) Bill, 2006, which has been introduced in Parliament, makes no mention of a 'creamy layer'.

1.11. The Oversight Committee finds it difficult to subscribe to this extreme view. In fact there are major implementation level implication where one set of initiatives will be required if the creamy layer is excluded from reservations and an entirely different set of initiatives will be required if creamy layer is allowed to avail reservations.

1.12. The study made in the Planning Commission takes a broad look at the status of the OBCs and is reproduced at Appendix 2.

1.13. In case it is decided not to exclude the 'creamy layer', the poorest among the OBCs will be placed at a disadvantage.

THE WAY FORWARD

7.1. As indicated earlier in this report, this opportunity for expansion, inclusion and excellence should only be the beginning of a larger process, which is to build a knowledge society in India and allow the country to take its rightful place in the comity of nations. Our recent economic growth and the values of knowledge and education carried forward by a billion diverse people, point to India's potential future as a knowledge society. Other countries that visualize a similar future have planned massive investments in order to enhance both the quality and quantity of higher education and research. China, for example, has made substantial increases in its allocation of resources of higher education. In the first phase, China has provided a grant of US $ 125 million to each of the 10 leading universities and US $ 225 million to Beijing and Tsinghua Universities. In the second phase, China proposes to provide additional grants to 30 universities, with the objective of having 100 high-quality universities in China in the 21st century and with 15% of its citizens in the age group 18-22 receiving tertiary education.

7.2. India has suffered in the past because of severe under investment in higher education. This has been caused partly by the thinking that looks at primary and higher education in an either or manner. It is very clear, however, that large public investment is needed in both sectors. As Prime Minister Dr. Manmohan Singh said, while launching the Knowledge Commission, "At the bottom of the knowledge pyramid, the challenge is one of improving access to primary education. At the top of the pyramid there is need to make our institutions of higher education and research world class. The time has come for India to embark on a second wave of nation building. Denied this investment, the youth will become a social and economic liability."

7.3. As indicated by the Prime Minister, we do need a second wave of nation building. If we do that seriously and earnestly, we will be in a position to develop human resources that are capable of utilizing available knowledge to create wealth and of generating new knowledge and innovation. If we do not, India would have lost out in the intensely competitive, globalized environment of today. It is beyond doubt or dispute that a country with a strong education foundation can have a much higher level of social and economic development. This report is merely a starting point in this direction. We need to draw up a much more comprehensive road map for the future, a vision document.

Index